BOSTON
Food Crawls

J.Q. Louise

TOURING *the* NEIGHBORHOODS
ONE BITE *&* LIBATION *at a* TIME

Globe Pequot
GUILFORD, CONNECTICUT

Globe
Pequot

An imprint of The Rowman & Littlefield Publishing Group, Inc,
4501 Forbes Blvd., Ste. 200
Lanham, MD 20706
www.rowman.com

Distributed by NATIONAL BOOK NETWORK

British Library Cataloguing in Publication Information available
Library of Congress Cataloging-in-Publication Data available

ISBN 978-1-4930-3426-0 (paperback)
ISBN 978-1-4930-3427-7 (e-book)

♾™ The paper used in this publication meets the minimum requirements
of American National Standard for Information Sciences—Permanence of
Paper for Printed Library Materials, ANSI/NISO Z39.48-1992

Printed in the United States of America

Contents

Foreword

Boston is an absolutely beautiful city. The beauty is not limited to its views. The neighborhoods, the people, and the food are all picture-perfect.

When I moved to Boston in 2009, I fell in love with the vibrancy of the city. It was exciting to explore each neighborhood and learn about the history behind each building. And that charm and vibrancy of the city has kept me here.

The food scene is incredible. Even in the past few years that I have been the Executive Chef at the Envoy, I've seen the city change and grow. As a chef, I definitely have a pulse on the food scene in town and I love the changes I am seeing. The diversity and quality of the restaurants opening up each year just keeps getting better and better and pushes me to think out of the box while still using local ingredients.

At my own restaurant I take inspiration from my Cuban background but also from all the amazing local farms and produce. I think that people respond to that passion and sense something exciting and new happening in the Seaport and throughout Boston.

When J.Q. told me she was writing this book, I was excited to see all the wonderful things happening in Boston wrapped up in one package. From the Seaport to Back Bay to the South End, there are so many talented chefs making great food in our beautiful neighborhoods. Boston deserves this book. We are a world-class city and J.Q. did an amazing job showcasing all that Boston's restaurant scene has to offer.

I am proud to call myself a Bostonian (by way of Miami) and I am proud to have been a part of the *Boston Food Crawls.* Read on to check out what each neighborhood has to offer!

Tatiana Rosana, Executive Chef
Outlook Kitchen and Bar &
Lookout Rooftop and Bar
The Envoy Hotel

Follow the Icons

 When you're crawling through Boston, everyone is a foodie, and every foodie is a photographer! This icon indicates only the absolute most photogenic spots that you must instagram while you're there.

 Look for this when there's something special to celebrate! These restaurants set the bar high for special occasions or simply add some glitz and glam to any night out.

 Follow this icon when you're crawling for cocktails. This symbol points out the establishments that are best known for their great drinks. The food never fails here, but make sure to come thirsty, too!

 This means that sweet treats are ahead. Bring your sweet tooth to these spots for dessert first (or second, or third).

 Boston is for brunch. Look for this icon when crawling with a crew that needs sweet and savory (or an excuse to drink before noon).

The Seaport

**Not Your Father's Fish Joint:
Lobster Sushi, Oysters & IPAs**

THE SEAPORT IN AND OF ITSELF IS A TESTAMENT TO "NEW" BOSTON. Once full of parking lots and piers, it is now one of the most desirable places in the city to live and work. Making up the area north of the Boston Convention Center between the Fort Point Channel and the Reserve Channel, the Seaport is close to downtown, Southie and the South End. With young professionals moving to the area and new high-rises going up every day, the Seaport is buzzing! In fact, many of Boston's companies, big and small, have made the Seaport their home. All this activity has brought a new energy to this beautiful area of the city. It is also among the most dynamic restaurant scenes in the city. From old stalwarts like the No Name to newcomers like the Outlook Kitchen, the Seaport is a must for someone looking to experience all that Boston has to offer. With fresh seafood, talented chefs, and beautiful views of Boston Harbor, it's easy to see why the Seaport is now a luxurious, waterfront neighborhood!

THE SEAPORT CRAWL

1. **Get your chowder fix at NO NAME**
   15½ FISH PIER ST. E., BOSTON, (617) 423-705, NONAMERESTAURANT.COM

2. **Go to the OUTLOOK KITCHEN AND THE LOOKOUT BAR in the Envoy Hotel for rooftop drinks and chic international cuisine**
   70 SLEEPER ST., BOSTON, (617) 338-3030, OUTLOOKKITCHENANDBAR.COM

3. **Stop by DRINK for the funkiest cocktails in town before your date night at MENTON**
   348 CONGRESS ST., BOSTON, (617) 695-1806, DRINKFORTPOINT.COM
   354 CONGRESS ST., BOSTON, (617)-737-0099, MENTONBOSTON.COM

4. **Get the girls (or boys) together for a sushi-filled night out at EMPIRE**
   1 MARINA PARK DR., BOSTON, (617) 295-0001, EMPIREBOSTON.COM

5. **Sip on something tasty while you play bocce at the LAWN ON D**
   420 D ST., BOSTON, (877) 393-3393, SIGNATUREBOSTON.COM/LAWN-ON-D

6. **Linger over the beautiful raw bar at ROW 34**
   383 CONGRESS ST., BOSTON, (617) 553-5900, ROW34.COM

7. **Sample some IPAs and fresh pretzels at the HARPOON headquarters**
   306 NORTHERN AVE., BOSTON, (617) 456-2322, HARPOONBREWERY.COM/BREWERIES/BOSTON

8. **Look at the boats while you feast on a lobster dinner at LEGAL HARBORSIDE**
   270 NORTHERN AVE., BOSTON, (617) 477-2900, LEGALSEAFOODS.COM

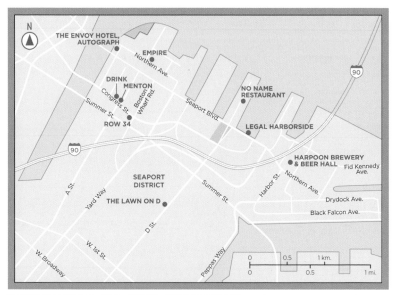

LET'S HEAD TO THE SEAPORT!

1 GET YOUR CHOWDER FIX AT NO NAME

Located directly on the "Fish Pier," right on Boston Harbor, the **NO NAME** has been dishing out fresh seafood since 1917. I still recommend it to anyone craving creamy fish chowder, but be prepared: this is a no-frills kind of place, which I would say ups its charm even more.

I have fond memories of dining here as a child with my family. The menu is straight-forward, separated into sections of broiled, fried, salads, sandwiches, appetizers, and desserts. What you see is what you get. Like I said, the No Name is perfect for anyone looking for classic seafood dishes. My "must-trys" are the Fish Chowder and the Fish and Chips.

Nowadays the Seaport is filled with many more dining options than there were in 1917. From the amazing Georges Bank Scallops at the Outlook Kitchen to the Black Bass Crudo at Menton, the Seaport is definitely inspired by its maritime roots. Some of the best dishes in the neighborhood still involve seafood.

 **GO TO THE OUTLOOK KITCHEN AND LOOKOUT BAR IN THE ENVOY HOTEL FOR ROOFTOP DRINKS AND CHIC INTERNATIONAL CUISINE**

The restaurant inside the Envoy Hotel, **OUTLOOK KITCHEN**, is a new classic. When Chef Tatiana Rosana took the helm in 2016, she upped the ante on the menu. Adding in fast favorites like the Georges Bank Scallops and Bay of Fundy Atlantic Salmon, the restaurant quickly became known for amazingly fresh ingredients and creative combinations.

My number one must-try at Outlook is the Georges Bank Scallops, with perfectly seared scallops, creamy lobster succotash, soft gnocchi, and a drizzle of basil oil—yum! These stellar dishes and more will keep you coming back again and again.

The Outlook Kitchen at the Envoy Hotel is truly a standout in the neighborhood because of this balance of respect and daring when it comes to the menu choices. By using local ingredients to create innovative dishes, the restaurant is able to strike a chord with Boston foodies.

However, the appetizer menu and bar bites are also standouts if you are looking for a quick snack after work or a little amuse bouche before you get your Saturday night started. In line with the traditions of the neighborhood, but also speaking to her heritage, Chef Rosana recently added to the menu a deliciously crispy Grilled Octopus dish that is also a must-try.

And when all that delicious food has you feeling good, head on up to Lookout Bar on the hotel's rooftop for a drink or two. The Envoy rooftop is definitely one of the hottest spots in town, great for after-work drinks or Saturday nights. With the combination of the view, the ambiance, and the creative list of cocktails, it's easy to see why it

"I wanted to respect the fisherman's culture of the Seaport while bringing in my own Cuban flair to the restaurant. I love bringing together different traditions and creating dishes that can truly tug on heartstrings."

— *Chef Tatiana Rosana*

is such a favorite. And if you want to keep the night going, head to Drink down the street for some more tasty libations.

STOP BY DRINK FOR THE FUNKIEST COCKTAILS IN TOWN BEFORE YOUR DATE NIGHT AT MENTON

Two completely different concepts that go hand in hand are Barbara Lynch's **DRINK** and **MENTON**. Drink is a subterranean cocktail bar, and Menton is one of the grand dames of Boston's food scene.

Drink speaks to the young professional population that is now so prevalent in the Seaport. There was an incessant need for fashionable watering holes in the neighborhood, and Drink led the way for the many others that have cropped up in the past few years. Drink is a cocktail bar with no cocktail list; instead, you just tell the knowledgeable bartenders what you like, and they whip up something tasty. Proving that a good bartender is worth his or her weight in gold, there is usually a line of people down the street waiting to get in each Friday and Saturday night. But there is an insider track to skip the line: if you dine at Menton first, the staff will reserve a spot for you downstairs at Drink and take you through the kitchen right to your seat at the bar.

While there is no menu, there are a few favorites that locals love, so a few of the drinks poured do have names:

1) Martinique Swizzle—Martinique rum, lime, sugar, absinthe
2) Fort Point—Benedictine, punt e mes, old overshoot rye

Drink is the perfect place to hang out before your dinner at Menton. As the flagship of Barbara Lynch's empire, Menton is special. With a tasting menu fit for a king, you will not be disappointed. However, be prepared: this 10-course experience, with wine pairings, runs around $300 per person. While most may have to reserve this treat for a special occasion, I will say that you won't be disappointed. The food, the service, the atmosphere—they are all exceptional.

Each dish is meticulously prepared—just look at the cross-hatching on that Black Bass Crudo (top right)!

They are so deliciously innovative, as well. They weren't joking with the name of one dessert; it truly is a "Floating Island" (second from top, right).

While the "Chef's Whim" menu is definitely the highlight of the restaurant, Menton also serves

"When I opened Menton in 2010, I could feel the neighborhood changing. The first high-rises were going up, startups were coming to the area, young professionals were moving in. The neighborhood had a new energy."

—Chef Barbara Lynch

lunch and offers an à la carte dinner menu. It even has a bar menu! So there are plenty of reasons to try out this amazing cuisine.

Our next stop is Empire, the best place in the Seaport for a big night out!

While **Drink** definitely reigns supreme in the cocktail department, the bartenders at **Menton**'s "Gold Bar" are no slouches either. Here is a recipe for one of their standbys:

Chelsea Swizzle:

1 oz caña brava rum
1 oz plantation 5-yr rum
¾ oz Demerara syrup
¾ oz lime juice
Angostura bitters float

Shake first 4 ingredients and strain over crushed ice into a high ball glass. Top with bitters. Garnish with mint and an orange twist.

4 GET THE GIRLS (OR BOYS) TOGETHER FOR A SUSHI NIGHT OUT AT EMPIRE

EMPIRE is something that the Seaport never saw coming. Part Asian fusion restaurant, part nightclub, it is perfect for a night out with your friends. You can start with a sushi dinner and then move over to the lounge for the rest of the night.

Empire is famous for its large-format drinks, namely the Big Kahuna (Grey Goose, Fresh Watermelon Punch, Mint & Ginger) and the Pineapple Mai Tai (choice of Classic with Bacardi 8 or White Mai Tai with Ciroc Pineapple). Get one of these bad boys to share over dinner. The fresh watermelon in the Big Kahuna pairs well with the flavorful sushi and other interesting small plates.

Some winners on the small plate side are the Hawaiian Style Poke and the Rice Bites.

And for entrees, you have to try the Alaskan Black Cod and the Korean Rubbed Sirloin.

But the real fun starts when you get to the sushi and the nigiri. Empire holds nothing back. If you love fun, fusion-focused sushi dishes, you will love what is coming out of the Empire kitchen.

One must-try is the nigiri surf and turf, which includes some tender waygu and lovely sockeye salmon.

After all that fun on your night out, some fresh air the next day could definitely do you some good. Recover outdoors at everyone's favorite lawn in the Seaport.

5

SIP ON SOMETHING TASTY WHILE YOU PLAY BOCCE AT THE LAWN ON D

The **LAWN ON D** is exactly what its name suggests: a lawn on D Street. But what you wouldn't know until you go there is that it is actually home to a lovely outdoor bar and all the yard games you could ask for. All cities need more outdoor space, and this patch of green among the brand-new skyscrapers and condo buildings is literally a breath of fresh air.

While seasonal, the Lawn on D is a family-friendly place to hang out. You can play bocce or lounge in an Adirondack chair with a cocktail while the kids run around.

The brightly colored lawn furniture is a cheery addition to this wonderful space. And I'm glad that they didn't make the Lawn on D 21+ because the Seaport is home to so many young families these days. Everyone deserves to have an outdoor space to enjoy in the warmer months.

Speaking of things to enjoy in the summer, raw bars are another go-to, and Row 34 has a fantastic one.

6

LINGER OVER THE BEAUTIFUL RAW BAR AT ROW 34

If you couldn't tell, the Seaport is the place to get great seafood in Boston. And that trend continues at **ROW 34**. With a raw bar to die for, Row 34 is for people who love oysters and appreciate when they are done right.

Whenever you visit Row 34, at least the first part of your meal is a no-brainer. You have to get some oysters on the half shell. If you don't know Wellfleet from Island Creek, the staff will help you put together the perfect fruits de mer platter. I know oysters can be intimidating, but it's just like choosing wine. There's really no wrong answer—it's all about your personal preference.

While oysters are certainly the star of the show, don't neglect the other raw members of the Row 34 family. The selection of crudos and ceviches is also extensive. I personally love the tuna crudo.

If you come to Row 34, chances are you like raw seafood, but if you have someone in your party who does not, there are plenty of cooked options as well. If you're visiting Boston, I recommend the lobster roll. Row 34 does a solid rendition of this New England classic: crispy bun; cold, succulent lobster; and just the right amount of mayo and spices. The lobster should always be the ruler of his domain, without anything else vying for too much power. Here that holds true.

While I love a good raw bar all year round, winter in Boston calls for something hearty after a meal on ice. Fresh pretzels and IPAs and our next stop, Harpoon, will warm up even the chilliest day out.

7

SAMPLE SOME IPAS AND FRESH PRETZELS AT THE HARPOON HEADQUARTERS

Yes, **HARPOON** is headquartered in Boston's very own Seaport. And you can visit the actual brewery, as well as sample some of its world-famous IPAs. The beer hall is a popular weekend hangout, especially in the winter when a warm pretzel and a cold IPA just seem to do the trick.

When you visit Harpoon, start with a tour of the brewery. Tours are held hourly, and tickets are only $5 each. You'll get to see where the beer is brewed and bottled. The majority of global production takes place right in this Boston location. At the end of the tour, you'll head to the tasting room, where everyone gets to sample the many different varieties offered by the brand. If you're lucky, one of the bartenders will show you some secret blends—mixes of two of the beers that create unique and fun new flavors.

And after the tour, head out to the beer hall for some more beer flights and a tasty giant pretzel. There are a few different choices for dips, but I always go with the Ale Mustard and Bacon Ranch.

Just up the street from Harpoon is the perfect way to wrap up your Seaport Crawl, Legal Harborside.

LOOK AT THE BOATS WHILE YOU FEAST ON A LOBSTER DINNER AT LEGAL HARBORSIDE

The perfect end to your food crawl of the Seaport is **LEGAL HARBORSIDE**. The flagship of the Legal Seafoods empire, Legal Harborside is the epitome of the modern Seaport. Updated classics with a view is the name of the game here.

Whenever I want a perfect lobster dinner with a cup of renowned clam chowder, I head to Legal Harborside. And I don't know about you, but I feel like lobster should always be eaten in the sea breeze. The restaurant's extensive patio allows for just that.

There are many new favorites at Legal Harborside, as well, like the Lobster Tempura Roll. This type of forward thinking is what has made Legal Harborside a new landmark since it opened in 2011.

Legal Harborside led the way for the transformation of the Seaport's dining scene. As the first new major development on Seaport Boulevard, the restaurant gave people working and living in Boston a reason to hike across the Fort Point Channel. This new influx of people was a harbinger of all the activity and life to come to the neighborhood.

Beacon Hill
Café Society

BEACON HILL HAS ALWAYS BEEN ONE OF MY FAVORITE NEIGHBORHOODS. Looking down on Boston Common and out at the Charles River, Beacon Hill is located right in the center of Boston. Its historic homes, cobblestone streets, and the lovely Charles Street, make it the absolute classic Boston neighborhood. It is a magical place, somehow both bustling and quiet. It's just a wonderful place to be. Once home to John Hancock, Charles Bulfinch, Robert Frost, and many other historical figures, it's no wonder Beacon Hill still carries itself with an aristocratic air. The stately homes in Louisburg Square, the gold dome on the State house, and the brownstones on Beacon Street add to the picturesque quality of the scene here. But don't think for one second that all that history means staid eateries. Beacon Hill residents certainly do love to eat out! That means the neighborhood is filled with cafes, fine dining and cocktail spots that are all worth a look!

THE BEACON HILL CRAWL

1. **Start off the day with a treat from** PANIFICIO
   144 CHARLES ST., BOSTON, (617) 227-4340, PANIFICIOBOSTON.COM

2. **Finish the day with a drink at the** LIBERTY HOTEL
   215 CHARLES ST., BOSTON, (617) 224-4000, LIBERTYHOTEL.COM

3. **Start the weekend with a date at** NO. 9 PARK
   9 PARK ST., BOSTON, (617) 742-9991, NO9PARK.COM

4. **Celebrate all that's good in the world at** MA MAISON
   272 CAMBRIDGE ST., BOSTON, (617) 725-8855, MAMAISONBOSTON.COM

5. **Relax like a Brahmin at the** BEACON HILL BISTRO
   25 CHARLES ST., BOSTON, (800) 640-3935, BEACONHILLHOTEL.COM/
   BOSTON-BISTRO

6. **Enjoy something different at** LALA ROKH
   97 MT. VERNON ST., BOSTON, (617) 720-5511, LALAROKH.COM

7. **Grab a beer with your buddies at** CARRIE NATION
   11 BEACON ST., BOSTON, (617) 227-3100, CARRIENATIONCOCKTAILCLUB.COM

8. **Bring your boss to** BIN 26 ENOTECA
   26 CHARLES ST., BOSTON, (617) 723-5939, BIN26.COM

9. **Spend an afternoon people watching from** TATTE
   70 CHARLES ST., BOSTON, (617) 723-5555, TATTEBAKERY.COM

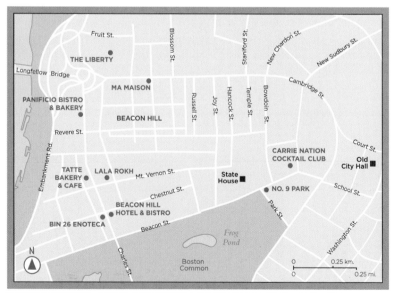

LET'S FIND OUT WHERE YOU SHOULD GO TO GRAB A BITE ON THE HILL!

1 START OFF THE DAY WITH A TREAT FROM PANIFICIO

A good bakery will never go out of style, and one that can do a solid latte with plenty of creamy foam is definitely here to stay. **PANIFICIO** is one of Beacon Hill's insider hotspots. If you don't live on the hill, you probably haven't heard of it. But you heard it here first: head to Panificio for some fantastic pastries and coffee. They also do a solid light brunch menu, by the way. I mean just look at that latte art—what more could you ask for?

The baristas know what they're doing, and the pastry case is filled with plenty of goodies. And to top all that off, the rustic wooden tables make for a super cozy place to relax for a bit before your day gets running. So whether you go for a giant cookie or a cinnamon stick, as long as you are enjoying it with a giant latte, your day is going to be just fine!

Just at the top of Charles Street, Panificio is a hop, skip, and a jump from the Charles MGH T stop, so pretend you're a local and head over tomorrow morning to start the day off on the right foot!

At the end of that great day, grab your coworkers and enjoy a cocktail at the Liberty Hotel.

2 FINISH THE DAY WITH A DRINK AT THE LIBERTY HOTEL

Finish off your day right around the corner at the **LIBERTY HOTEL**. Consistently one of the hottest cocktail spots around, the Liberty is the place to see and be seen on Beacon Hill. The creative cocktails and fun vibe will let you unwind in the coolest manner possible. And during the summer the Liberty patio is a lovely spot to enjoy the beautiful Boston nights.

Now for all you out-of-towners who might not understand just why the Liberty is so high on the cool-o-meter, it was once known as the Charles Street Jail and, as such, has kept a little bit of that heritage alive. You can still go to the "Clink," except now instead of inmates you'll see some fabulously kind waiters and waitresses. Today the Clink is one of the restaurants on the property; it's a great place to enjoy an amazing cocktail and some fitting décor as well!

After happy hour, take your special someone to No. 9 Park for a truly special meal.

3

START THE WEEKEND WITH A DATE AT NO. 9 PARK

Another feather in Barbara Lynch's cap, **NO. 9 PARK** is the crown jewel of Beacon Hill fine dining. If you are looking for a chic and tasty date night on the hill, head to No. 9. Trust me, Barbara will take care of you. Along the same lines as her other restaurants, No. 9's cuisine is well plated, beautifully executed, and a delight to the taste buds. Here you have to go for the tasting menu if you have time, but if not, a quick bite at the bar isn't a bad idea either. Oh and don't worry, the wine list and drink menu manage to keep up with the food, which is no small feat!

Start off the night with some pasta or even (do I dare?) fondue, and then move on to a lovely piece of fish. Finish your meal with a perfectly crafted dessert. The experience at No. 9 never disappoints.

This place reminds me of some of those tiny boutique hotels in London. You walk in and just feel like everyone is on a clandestine mission. The atmosphere is dark and sophisticated—in a word, very Beacon Hill.

So take a stroll up the hill, look for the understated No. 9 sign, and head on in. You're in for a treat!

Next up, is another one of my favorites, Ma Maison, a classic French bistro right here in Boston.

4 CELEBRATE ALL THAT'S GOOD IN THE WORLD AT MA MAISON

Chef Jacky Robert does it again with his latest addition, MA MAISON. Located on the back side of Beacon Hill, Ma Maison is everything you could ask of a French bistro. They do the classics, and they do them well.

I give any new French restaurant I'm trying the same test. I call it the bread-and-butter test. The bread should be crispy on the outside and soft on the inside, and the butter should be served room temperature. After all, if you can't get the staples right, what can you do? Ma Maison passed my test with flying colors.

And when you move on to some more complicated things, like the foie gras or the tartare, Ma Maison more than meets expectations. It exceeds them. The tartare is fresh and tasty, and the foie gras is enticing and rich. This is the place to go if you want to have a beautiful dinner in a setting that will make you feel like you're back in Paris. A true Parisian bistro is warm, relaxing, and homey, and Chef Robert is spot on with Ma Maison. Beacon Hill deserves a warm, beautiful neighborhood bistro straight out of Paris. So, leave all your problems at the door and enter Jacky's Maison.

The pro tip here is go for the wine pairing with the foie gras. You will not be disappointed. And do not skip dessert! The French know how to slow down and enjoy their meals, and that includes multiple courses, so please don't skimp on time or calories.

While I'm sure Chef Jacky will leave you stuffed, keep up your good eats streak by heading to the Beacon Hill Bistro roof deck.

5

RELAX LIKE A BRAHMIN AT THE BEACON HILL BISTRO

The **BEACON HILL HOTEL AND BISTRO** is a Charles Street mainstay. The hotel itself is a lovely place to stay in the heart of Boston, with your fingers solidly on the pulse of Beacon Hill. And the Bistro follows suit. Whether you come in for dinner or brunch, you'll breathe a sigh of relief as you step into the civility that is the restaurant. Every time I come here for brunch, I get the urge to pick up a newspaper and linger over my cappuccino just a little bit longer than I normally would. Be the Brahmin you always knew you could be and enjoy the ambiance of the BHB.

Oh and if you're looking for another insider tip, head to the roof deck. Yes, Beacon Hill Hotel and Bistro has a roof deck—a well-kept secret around these parts!

A sunny respite in a busy world, the roof deck is open all day during nice weather. And you can enjoy any meal up there. So order a drink or the tartare and take in the view of the gorgeous Charles Street below. With bartenders who push the envelope each season, the drink list is constantly changing, so ask what's new. I'm sure they will bring out something amazing. Pairing one of these fantastic concoctions with a tasty bite from either the lunch or dinner menu will be the best decision you make all day!

Well, except for going to Lala Rokh for some Persian fare that evening!

6

ENJOY SOMETHING DIFFERENT AT LALA ROKH

In a neighborhood filled with cafés, **LALA ROKH** is an amazing departure. Serving up authentic and delicious Persian cuisine, this restaurant will break you out of your take-out rut in an instant. Whatever dish you choose, the flavors, spices, and sauces will mesmerize you. This is my absolute favorite Persian spot in town and is a must-try for both locals and out-of-towers.

A deep understanding of flavor profiles is so important for these dishes, and Lala Rokh hits it out of the park. The quail is worth the walk up the hill all on its own!

So break out of your routine and head to Beacon Hill for a tasty Middle Eastern meal at Lala Rokh. Located just off Charles Street, the restaurant is a great place to discuss all the fab shopping you did in the neighborhood.

Let's head to Carrie Nation for a night cap.

7 GRAB A BEER WITH YOUR BUDDIES AT CARRIE NATION

Foodies usually dismiss bars on Beacon Hill because they think of them as bastions of antique cocktails and stale nachos, but **CARRIE NATION** breaks that stereotype. With a vivacious bartender whipping up some creative brews and a menu made for sharing, Carrie Nation is a spot to go when you want to just sit somewhere and feel like everybody knows your name.

There is something to be said for having the occasional dinner at the bar. Just order a classic like the baked chicken or roasted salmon and pair it with something from behind the bar, then sit back and enjoy the evening. Simple can be good.

And if simple isn't what you're going for, Carrie Nation also has a secret back room where you can kick it up a notch. With pool tables, dark lighting, and a wonderful speakeasy vibe, it's no wonder so many cool events are held here. Whether you come in for a drink, for dinner, or for the speakeasy, Carrie Nation is always a good time.

Swap your sneakers for stilettos for the next stop, Bin 26 Enoteca on Charles Street.

Pair wine and cheese like a pro
Ordering the right wine can make the most seasoned food crawlers feel lost. Add in the whole cheese palate, and the intimidation factor might just be enough to scare anyone out of an extra special dining experience. Never fear, we've got you covered.

Remember these few classic pairings and prepare to impress at Bin 26 Enoteca.

MANCHEGO with
CHIANTI
CLASSICO

PECORINO with
VALPOLICELLA

TALEGGIO with
PINOT BLANC

8

BRING YOUR BOSS TO BIN 26 ENOTECA

The sister restaurant to Lala Rokh, **BIN 26 ENOTECA** is not your average wine bar. With things like Cocoa Tagliatelle on the menu, they go a different direction while maintaining that neighborhood wine bar tradition of offering simple, tasty food and plenty of wine.

My number one pick here is the ThreeMisu, a classic tiramisu with tiramisu ice cream and cream sauce, so you get the classic in three preparations. You seriously cannot leave without trying this!

But I think all our mothers would be disappointed in us if we started with dessert, so begin with a lovely selection from the cheese menu, then perhaps move on to pasta, and finally indulge in dessert.

Bin 26 is a great choice for date night, girls' night out, or even a dinner with the boss or co-workers. It can be what you want it to be: a drink at the bar, a romantic night in the dining room, or an evening of watching out the window as people pass by on Charles Street.

Being a wine bar, ask your server all about the wine and cheese pairings that they recommend. They have a fab formaggi menu, so try a few things out the next time you stop in!

9

SPEND AN AFTERNOON PEOPLE WATCHING FROM TATTE

And finally, last but certainly not least, head to **TATTE** for an afternoon of people watching on their glorious Charles Street patio. Everything is superb here. Grab a latte and a pastry or a lemonade and a salad—it's exactly what you'd want from such a local favorite.

A local café brand, Tatte does mornings right with flaky pastry, creamy lattes, and indulgent breakfast sandwiches.

One of my all-time favorite Beacon Hill pastimes is posting up on the Tatte patio, Matcha latte in hand, to enjoy the afternoon. Boston is probably the most European city in America, and I think we all need to start enjoying that fact a little bit more. Nothing is more productive than an afternoon at a café; there's friends to catch up with, warm sun to soak up, and plenty of books to read. Take some me time and head to Tatte.

> "When visiting Tatte, I hope Bostonians take a moment to enjoy and treat themselves. Boston has embraced us with open arms, and it makes me so happy that we are a part of so many peoples' lives."
>
> — *Tzurit Or, Founder of Tatte*

The Back Bay

Classy but Sassy:
Perfect for Your Mother or Your Mistress

THE BACK BAY IS BOSTON'S TONIEST NEIGHBORHOOD. From the gorgeous brownstones on Commonwealth Avenue to the shops on Newbury Street to the views of the Esplanade, Back Bay has it all. Both a chic residential neighborhood and a busy business center, the Back Bay is bustling day and night. For years there were only a few culinary mainstays in the neighborhood, but recently the area has gotten a lot more hip. Now you can find raw bars, Asian fusion eateries, and classic hangouts amongst its famous streets. There is really something for everyone in the Back Bay. A safe bet for either a Sunday brunch with the girls or a five course-tasting menu with your special someone, this neighborhood holds its own in the world of Boston foodies. Back Bay chefs definitely know what they are doing, so this is not a neighborhood to skip on your culinary tour of Boston! Back Bay-ers have some refined pallets, so even big-name chefs step up their game when they come to this part of town.

THE BACK BAY CRAWL

1. **Treat yourself to something amazing at L'ESPALIER**
   774 BOYLSTON ST., BOSTON, (617) 262-3023, LESPALIER.COM

2. **Head to my favorite steakhouse in town, GRILL 23**
   161 BERKELEY ST., BOSTON, (617) 542-2255, GRILL23.COM

3. **Refresh at SELECT OYSTER BAR after a day of shopping**
   50 GLOUCESTER ST., BOSTON, (857) 239-8064, SELECTBOSTON.COM

4. **Impress your out-of-town friends with the view at the TOP OF THE HUB**
   800 BOYLSTON ST., BOSTON, (617) 536-1775, TOPOFTHEHUB.NET

5. **Grabs drinks with your Tinder match at BAR BOULUD**
   776 BOYLSTON ST., BOSTON, (617) 535-8800, MANDARINORIENTAL.COM

6. **Gorge on uni at UNI**
   370 A COMMONWEALTH AVE., BOSTON, (617) 536-7200, UNI-BOSTON.COM

7. **Pretend you're in Brooklyn and feast on a funky tasting menu at ASTA**
   47 MASSACHUSETTS AVE., BOSTON, (617) 585-9575, ASTABOSTON.COM

8. **Go to DEUXAVE for date night**
   371 COMMONWEALTH AVE., BOSTON, (617) 517-5915, DEUXAVE.COM

9. **Fill up at MET BACK BAY before shopping till you drop**
   279 DARTMOUTH ST., BOSTON, (617) 267-0451, METBACKBAY.COM

10. **Share a family-sized feast at OAK LONG BAR + KITCHEN**
    138 ST. JAMES AVE., BOSTON, (617) 585-7222, OAKLONGBARKITCHEN.COM

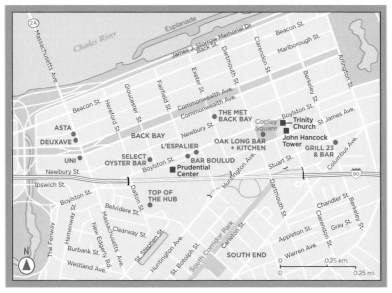

SO LET'S TAKE A STROLL THROUGH THE BACK BAY!

1

TREAT YOURSELF TO SOMETHING AMAZING AT L'ESPALIER

L'ESPALIER remains the gold standard in the Boston food world. The service, the cheese cart, the wine selection, and the food are all exemplary. But what really sets L'Espalier apart for me is the genuine love for fine dining that the restaurant exudes from the moment you step in to the moment you're handed a madeleine on your way out the door.

My absolute favorite time to dine at L'Espalier is on Marathon Monday. The restaurant is located close to the finish line, and since it's on the second floor you have the perfect bird's-eye view of all the excitement. I cannot think of a more sophisticated way to enjoy such a big day in Boston. And it isn't impossible to score one of these reservations, so I like to think that this is still an insider's tip (at least for now). On Marathon Monday L'Espalier offers a special lunch menu, usually including one cocktail. It's an amazing deal for the experience. Once you've had a Marathon Monday at L'Espalier, there's no going back. I've been going for the past 3 years, and I plan on continuing that tradition.

Now for the food. You really can't go wrong. Each dish is exquisite. Ask the sommelier for wine pairings to match; you'll be equally impressed.

But the true distinction on the menu is the cheese cart. I can say without a doubt that L'Espalier has the best cheese selection and cheese plate in

Boston. In fact my first visit to L'Espalier was on my 21st birthday for cocktails and cheese in the salon overlooking Boylston Street. Enjoying drinks and snacks in the lounge area of the restaurant is a lovely way to start or finish any evening. L'Espalier is one of Boston's true gems, and the city is honored to have such a high-caliber restaurant that has managed to stay relevant with the times.

And after all that cheese, if you are in the mood for a juicy steak, head to Grill 23.

2 HEAD TO MY FAVORITE STEAKHOUSE IN TOWN, GRILL 23

Say what you will about the humble steakhouse, but once in a while you just want a piece of meat cooked to perfection paired with a beautiful glass of wine. If that's what you're feeling at the moment, head over to GRILL 23. It's a place to go for oysters, a martini, and a rib eye. They do the classics well, and the staff is ready and more than willing to tell you all about them.

Grill 23 is definitely my favorite steakhouse in Boston. With a buzzing scene, juicy steaks, and a gigantic piece of cake for dessert, your once-a-year treat will be worth it!

Oftentimes the sommelier is the one who will make or break your meal, and at Grill 23 they certainly make it. From Taittinger to obscure California reds, the sommeliers will ensure you enjoy a match made in heaven. So not only will you walk out fat and happy, but you will leave with a little extra wine knowledge as well.

There are so many cuts of steak available, and Grill 23 offers the best of the best.

"I love fresh. And that's the reason I knew I had to start Select. When you serve things raw, they have to be perfect—there is nothing to cover it up. And I love that challenge."

— Michael Serpa,
chef/owner

3

REFRESH AT SELECT OYSTER BAR AFTER A DAY OF SHOPPING

Since you probably shouldn't be eating steaks every night, head to **SELECT OYSTER BAR** all the way down on Gloucester Street after a day of shopping on Newbury Street. This place knows its way around everything raw—oysters, tartare, crudo, you name it. These are the house specialties. And when you pair any of those with a crisp white wine, you're set up for the best afternoon ever.

Oh and they do a killer avocado toast, too! Talk about a refreshing meal: oysters, crudo, and avocado toast. Does it get any better or more Instagrammable than that? I don't think so. Chef Michael Serpa left Neptune Oyster in the North End to pursue his dream of opening up his own restaurant in order to deliver the best fresh ingredients to his patrons, and he is doing exactly that at Select.

4 IMPRESS YOUR OUT-OF-TOWN FRIENDS WITH THE VIEW AT THE TOP OF THE HUB

The award for best view has to go to the **TOP OF THE HUB**. Located on the 52nd floor of the Prudential Building, the restaurant has been going strong since 1952. And any restaurant with that type of longevity has to be doing something right. With fun dishes and a beautiful atmosphere, it's hard not to have a good time at the Top. I mean this could be your dinner view (above).

Yes, it is a tourist attraction, so occasionally there will be some under-dressed folks at the bar, but typically in the main dining room there is still a formality that most diners respect. And if you are just trying to have a good time, there is always the lounge side, which is a little more dressed down and closer to the live music offered on weekends.

My recommendation for dining at the Top is to try to get in for its express Prix Fixe lunch during the week. You'll love the executive dining room vibe, and the views during the day are spectacular. You can literally see for miles. But the sunsets are also fantastic, so really there is never a wrong time to dine at the Hub.

Oh and if you have visitors from out of town who are new to Boston, this will most definitely impress them and give them a chance to appreciate the beautiful city where we live.

5

GRAB DRINKS WITH YOUR TINDER MATCH AT BAR BOULUD

While the Top of the Hub has turned into a much more family-friendly place over the years, if you are looking for a sexier atmosphere, head to the nearby **BAR BOULUD**. The first Boston outpost from the famous Daniel Boulud, Bar Boulud is located on the ground floor of the Mandarin Oriental on Boylston Street, right next to the iconic Prudential Tower.

The location is prime for a Saturday night Tinder date, and the bar is fun enough to hang there with friends. But what will keep you coming back again and again are the French classics for which Chef Boulud is known.

And his innovative takes on old classics are so refreshing. The steak tartare, escargot, and steak frites are amazing throwbacks. I am obsessed!

The next stop is home to another famous chef, albeit a local one, Ken Oringer of Uni.

 GORGE ON UNI AT UNI

As its name suggests, **UNI** has an amazing uni dish. Well actually an "uni spoon," and if you are only going to have one dish there, that must be it. Located at the far end of Back Bay, at the intersection of Commonwealth and Massachusetts Avenues, Uni is inside the Elliott Hotel and is helmed by Ken Originer.

With a menu filled with creative maki rolls and Asian-inspired masterpieces, Uni is a true "foodie" haven. Even if you're the person who has tried everything, come to Uni and you will try something new.

Each plate is a work of art. The Spanish sea bass, spicy tuna, and foie gras tataki are perfect and taste even better.

> "Uni is such a versatile ingredient. My favorite way to use it is in the uni spoon, which has osetra caviar, quail egg yolk, yuzu. It's become a staple not only at Uni, but Toro as well. The balance of these dynamic flavors packs a memorable punch."
>
> —Ken Oringer, chef

The dark and mysterious vibe of the restaurant makes any meal there feel like a clandestine rendezvous. So if an old friend is in town and loves sushi, bring them here and you'll be sure to have a great time.

Tired from making all those a la carte choices? Give your brain a break just up the street on Mass. Ave. with the funky, cool set menu at Asta.

7

PRETEND YOU'RE IN BROOKLYN AND FEAST ON A FUNKY TASTING MENU AT ASTA

I am so proud of Boston because we have some restaurants that are truly pushing the envelope when it comes to concepts and menus these days. Task ASTA for example. Each night they offer just a tasting menu. You have 2 choices: either a 5-course set or an 8-course set. And once you make that choice, you are in for a wild ride.

When I last visited I did the 5-course menu, and it was very vegetable-forward, which I liked. I don't think there is another restaurant in town doing this sort of thing right now. For example, just look at that beauty, above right.

No other menu in Boston has that on there. And the fact that they offer only a tasting menu shows a unique type of bravery; they are saying each night that they 100 percent stand behind the ingredients they have sourced and the combinations they've put together. I like that, and I'm sure you will too. This is another "foodie" type of establishment. You have to have at least a slight adventurous streak to commit to a set menu, so get out of your comfort zone and give it a try.

For trendy bites a la carte, the nearby Deuxave has you covered.

8

GO TO DEUXAVE FOR DATE NIGHT

DEUXAVE was a trendsetter when Chef Coombs and Brian Piccini came to the neighborhood in 2010. Boston was entering a new era. We were coming out of the recession, younger people were starting to stay in town after graduating from college, and generally our palates were getting more sophisticated. The term "modern French" was starting to mean something around here, and Deuxave was a big part of that.

Today you should visit Deuxave if you want a tranquil date night or just to lounge on the patio in the summertime.

A dish like the "Night Moves" Lobster Gnocchi will make you forget all your troubles, especially when you pair it with a tasty libation from the seasonal drink menu.

And then move on to mains. Whether you are a meat or fish lover, they've got you covered. Dishes like the Pan-Seared Halibut and the Spiced Long Island Duck Breast delight.

Besides, fine dining, the Back Bay is also known as the shopping mecca of Boston, so of course you need a spot on Newbury to recharge your batteries during a shopping spree! Met Back Bay is always my go to.

9

FILL UP AT MET BACK BAY
BEFORE SHOPPING TILL YOU DROP

MET BACK BAY is my favorite boozy brunch on Newbury. Just take a look at the Bloody Marys! They could be your meal: they literally have a burger on top!

And if you're still hungry after that, fill the table with brunch plates to share and swap. Try the Eggs & Biscuit Benedict, the indulgent French toast, or the Truffled Croque Madame. There is no chance you will leave hungry, so you better come to Met ready to eat.

If you need a little more of a pick-me-up, pair any of these meals with one of the several coffee-themed cocktails on the brunch menu. And if you are still needing more, finish off with the healthy Green Goddess salad.

Met is also a fabulous spot for people watching. Located right on Newbury Street, whether you sit inside or outside, you can watch the world go by as you enjoy your delicious meal.

Seating for a big family dinner isn't always easy to find. If you're touring the Back Bay with the whole clan, head to Oak Long Bar + Kitchen inside the Fairmont Copley Hotel for some family-sized fun.

10

SHARE A FAMILY-SIZED FEAST AT OAK LONG BAR + KITCHEN

Located inside the Fairmont Copley Hotel, the **OAK LONG BAR + KITCHEN**, has always been one of my favorites. The location is prime—right in Copley Square—and Oak Long Bar is a stylish place to meet some old friends for a cocktail after work or to gather for a big family dinner.

The restaurant is moving toward sharable plates and family-style menus. Things like this family-sized roast chicken, for instance, could feed an army.

Oak is also good for brunch. It serves the best monkey bread I've ever had, and combined with a creamy cappuccino, my day was off to a fantastic start. Oh and that Lobster Benny didn't hurt either!

Whether you come in for brunch, drinks, or dinner, Oak Long Bar will brighten up your day and fill your stomach.

The South End

Take an Uber Because You're Going to Boozy Brunch

NOT TO BE CONFUSED WITH "SOUTH BOSTON," i.e. "Southie," the South End is adjacent to the Back Bay. Historically one of the most diverse neighborhoods in Boston proper, the South End is now home to amazing restaurants across cuisines. From French bistros to Asian fusion fare, the tone of the South End is trendy, stylish, rosé-all-day culture. Whenever I want brunch, my go-to neighborhood is the South End. With so many amazing choices, the South End is bound to please. Boston flipped the brunch switch a few years ago and hasn't looked back. The South End started all of that. From Metropolis to Aquitaine and Frenchie to the South End Buttery, and honestly to every restaurant in this chapter, you are guaranteed to find your next Sunday morning spot in this neck of the woods. After you've been in for omelets and mimosas, I recommend coming back in the evening for more tasty creations, the food in the South End is that good! Let's get to crawling!

THE SOUTH END CRAWL

1. Lounge at **METROPOLIS**, my favorite bistro in town
   548 TREMONT ST., BOSTON, (617) 247-2931, METROPOLISBOSTON.COM

2. Take a trip to Paris at **FRENCHIE WINE BISTRO** for some frosè
   560 TREMONT ST., BOSTON, (857) 233-5941, FRENCHIEBOSTON.COM

3. Say hola at **TORO** for tapas
   1704 WASHINGTON ST., BOSTON, (617) 536-4300, TORO-RESTAURANT.COM

4. Grab brunch with the girls at **AQUITAINE**
   569 TREMONT ST., BOSTON, (617) 424-8577, AQUITAINEBOSTON.COM

5. Sip on lattes and snack on cupcakes at **SOUTH END BUTTERY**
   314 SHAWMUT AVE., BOSTON, (617) 482-1015, SOUTHENDBUTTERY.COM

6. Enjoy reimagined Roman dishes at **CINQUECENTO ROMAN TRATTORIA**
   500 HARRISON AVE., BOSTON, (617) 338-9500, CINQUECENTOBOSTON.COM

7. Dine at **BANYAN BAR + REFUGE**, the trendiest fusion spot in the neighborhood
   553 TREMONT ST., BOSTON, (617) 556-4211, BANYANBOSTON.COM

8. Relax with some comfort food at **FIVE HORSES TAVERN**
   535 COLUMBUS AVE., BOSTON, (617) 936-3930, FIVEHORSESTAVERN.COM

9. Take your new special someone for drinks at the **GALLOWS**
   1395 WASHINGTON ST., BOSTON, (617) 425-0200, THEGALLOWSBOSTON.COM

10. Head to **LION'S TAIL** for the best of the Ink Block
    354 HARRISON AVE., BOSTON, (857) 239-9276, LIONSTAILBOSTON.COM

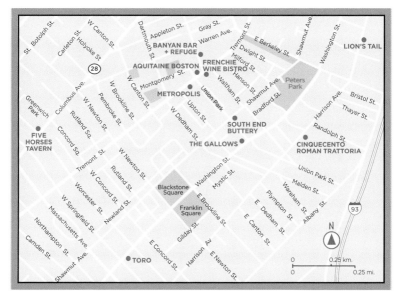

LET'S HEAD TO THE SOUTH END!

1

LOUNGE AT METROPOLIS, MY FAVORITE BISTRO IN TOWN

If there is one thing you can count on in the South End, it's the bistro. And while there are many, **METROPOLIS** is my go-to. When I'm in the mood for some roasted scallops or a grilled duck breast, I head down to Tremont Street.

Metropolis has that French bistro vibe, with its close quarters and comfortable lighting; it's the perfect place for a date, a business lunch, a family dinner, or a drink with a friend. In other words, anything—the mark of a true bistro.

The wines by the glass rarely disappoint, and in the summertime they put out a few select rosés that are particularly trustworthy. That expertly selected wine paired with the Summer Burrata on Toast is the perfect way to start any meal! To keep the French vibes going, make your next stop Frenchie, just up the street.

2 TAKE A TRIP TO PARIS WITH FRENCHIE WINE BISTRO FOR SOME FROSÈ

I was so happy to see that a new French bistro opened up at the intersection of Clarendon and Tremont Streets. **FRENCHIE WINE BISTRO** is just that: French. It's owned by Sandrine Rossi and Loïc Le Garrec of Petit Robert. And they know what they're doing. French transplants, they do the classics and do them well. The steak frites are a must, as are the steak tartare and moules frites. If you are craving some classic, well-executed French food, Frenchie is the place to go. You won't be disappointed.

Like I said, the South End has its fair share of bistros, but Frenchie is so refreshing because it's just a French bistro, not combined with any other theme or idea. As the name suggests, all they do is French. The servers are French, the food is French, and the owners are French. If your inner Francophile needs to emerge, head over to Frenchie.

"I'm so happy to see that Frenchie has received such a warm welcome in the South End. We wanted to bring some Parisian flair to the neighborhood, and I think we have."

— Sandrine Rossi, co-owner

The bright design, the patio, and the bar all make for a buzzing atmosphere, and in the summertime there is even another star: the frozè. With several different flavors offered each day, they are always crowd pleasers. If you head to Frenchie on a summer day, order a glass of frozè, sit on the patio, and watch the stylish crowds go by on Tremont Street. After all, it's the French way!

But the Spanish do know a thing or two about food as well, so be sure to make some time for tapas at Toro too!

WHAT IS A PORRON?

A porron is a communal drinking vessel from Spain. With a narrow top, similar to a wine bottle's, you can cork these things. But the bottom gets wider, more similar to a decanter, and then there is the conical spout. Basically, this is the Spanish way of making sure everyone is having a good time.

How does one use this, you are probably asking?

Well, you simply grab the wine bottle-esque top, lean back, and guzzle some wine as it shoots out from the spout. Basically, this thing is a recipe for a fun time. Pair a porron with some tapas and your evening is made.

3 SAY HOLA AT TORO FOR TAPAS

Ken Oringner and Jamie Bissonette are local celebrities, and **TORO** is one of their many bedrocks. Located deep in the South End, Toro has become a cult favorite over the years. Famously refusing to take reservations, the wait times can be immense on the weekends, but trust me, as soon as your street corn arrives at the table you'll know the wait was worth it.

Each dish is exactly as tapas should be: beautiful, tasty, share-worthy, and amazing.

From the famous street corn to the paella to the prosciutto board, Toro delights the taste buds with each bite.

At the heart of a good tapas meal is the sharing of all plates. And the reason Toro has been able to instill this feeling into the restaurant so well

> "Toro has maintained its appeal all this time because we refuse to stop having fun there. We never stop pushing for change and development in the kitchen. Our staff is so fantastic and is committed to excellent service, and I think the guests can genuinely feel that."
>
> — *Jamie Bissonette,*
> *chef/partner*

is that each dish looks so enticing that everyone at the table will be dying to try a bite!

The drinks program is also fabulous. With a seasonal drink menu, the cocktails often pair exceptionally with the dishes. But one constant that you just have to get if you stop by Toro is a Porron. A Porron is a Spanish wine pitcher that you drink from directly. Trust me, you will see guests pouring wine into their mouths from a Porron at some point in the evening!

After a night of pouring the porron, you might need a recovery brunch, and Aquitaine is just the South End spot for that!

4 GRAB BRUNCH WITH THE GIRLS AT AQUITAINE

AQUITAINE is one of those tried-and-true brunch spots on Tremont Street. Having recently undergone a complete facelift, the dining room and bar are perfect for debriefing with the girls after a night out.

The drinks program is magnificent. Your palate will be delighted by the creative offerings from the bar. With frequent new additions to the cocktail menu, you will always come in to something new.

Pair your drinks with some tasty concoctions from the kitchen, and your meal is sure to be a great start to your day! The delicate but decadent salads are a hit anytime of day or night.

You have to come to Aquitaine with an appetite because everything on the menu sounds so delectable. You won't be able to make up your mind on the ever-present brunch dilemma: sweet or savory? I usually go with a little bit of both!

Classics like the waffles or eggs benedict are always solid choices, but the more unique offerings are just as tasty.

Head to the nearby South End Buttery for some extra fuel for the road.

5

SIP ON LATTES AND SNACK ON CUPCAKES AT SOUTH END BUTTERY

The **SOUTH END BUTTERY** is an institution. Located in the heart of the ever-stylish Union Park neighborhood, South End Buttery does it all: part café, part coffeehouse, part bistro. Whether you are running to work and want to grab a latte and a pastry or are looking to linger on Friday night for a nice meal, South End Buttery is sure to please.

When I'm in the mood for a tasty sandwich and salad, South End Buttery is my café of choice in the South End. A few notches above any chain nearby, the eatery charms everyone who walks in. And you can tell it's such an important neighborhood institution because the warmth with which regulars and newbies are greeted by the staff speaks to the level of care they put into each interaction.

Is there anything that can turn a day around better than a delicious sandwich and salad? Sometimes all you need to get through the day is a tasty lunch, and the South End Buttery is the place to cure all those daily annoyances.

Plan ahead and make a dinner reservation at my favorite South End trattoria, Cinquecento.

ENJOY REIMAGINED ROMAN DISHES AT CINQUECENTO ROMAN TRATTORIA

It seems that Boston is reinventing what the term "Italian restaurant" means. No more generic red sauce and spaghetti joints. Regionally inspired haunts are popping up all over town, from Capo in Southie and now **CINQUECENTO ROMAN TRATTORIA** in the South End. A contemporary neighborhood spot, Cinquecento tries to capture the essence of the Roman trattoria. And while it might look a lot different physically than all the Roman trattorias I've ever been to, it certainly exudes that same energy and flavor you would expect to find in one.

From the Summer Burrata Crostini to the Prosciutto-Wrapped Veal Tenderloin and Roasted Octopus, the flavors and love are there. When it comes to Roman food, these are the main ingredients.

The Italian flavors and feeling give the area some variety, which is exactly what makes the South End such a foodie neighborhood. Oh and it doesn't hurt that Cinquecento also has one of the largest outdoor patios in town, where it hosts fun events all summer long! Since the restaurant is set back off the main street, the patio is like an urban oasis. You'll feel a million miles away from it all.

But if you want to be in the thick of it, the place for you is Banyan Bar + Refuge, our next stop on the South End crawl.

7

DINE AT BANYAN BAR + REFUGE, THE TRENDIEST FUSION SPOT IN THE NEIGHBORHOOD

Boston foodies mourned the departure of the Hamersley Bistro with great sadness, but when a new Asian-fusion hotspot, **BANYAN BAR + REFUGE**, opened in its place, that weight was lifted.

Banyan was the injection of different that the South End needed. While I love the French bistro dearly, variety certainly is the spice of life, and Banyan delivers just that.

From Rock Shrimp Bao with Papaya Slaw to Charred Shishitos with Ranch, the menu pushes the boundaries in the most unexpected places. And it does so successfully! But Banyan also knows when to keep things straightforward, like with the Salmon Poke—just some well-prepared fresh ingredients.

Oh and the drinks are out of this world! They're fun, tasty, and unexpected. Two things that you won't find anywhere else in town: the Beer Slushie and the cute little single-serve portions of sake. Banyan is a place to see and be seen, as well as a place to eat and enjoy. And that vibe is so South End, which explains why this place was such an instant hit.

When you're in the mood for some straightforward comfort food, our next stop will satisfy your craving, Five Horses Tavern.

RELAX WITH SOME COMFORT FOOD AT FIVE HORSES TAVERN

I like a 10-course-tasting menu with wine parings just as much as the next girl, but sometimes after a long day all you want is some mac and cheese and roasted chicken. And the place to get that is **FIVE HORSES TAVERN**.

The name of the game here is well-executed comfort food. Thoughtfully conceived dishes combined with friendly service and a roomy patio make for a wonderful meal.

Everything from the fried chicken salad to the burger to the roasted chicken is just perfect. It all reminds you of mom's cooking but still feels like a treat. Just off a quaint residential area behind the Prudential Building, Five Horses Tavern is like a dream neighborhood pub.

Truly a hidden gem, the Five Horses Tavern must be the best-kept secret in Boston. Columbus Avenue locals have been keeping it to themselves this whole time! Oh and be sure to bring any beer lovers in your life with you because to top it all off, Five Horses has one of the most expansive beer collections in town!

Next stop, the Gallows has got after-dinner drinks covered.

 9

TAKE YOUR NEW SPECIAL SOMEONE FOR DRINKS AT THE GALLOWS

Sexy, dark, and mysterious, the **GALLOWS** is the spot for date night. The chic bar area is the place to be. With fun cocktails and satisfying bar food to match, the Gallows is where you should go when you're tired of your old standbys.

While not for the calorie conscious, the menu has plenty of fun creations that are the perfect Friday night treat. Things like Pork Belly Pinxtos and Fried Cheese Balls are the perfect parings for the strong pours coming from the bar.

And if you have a heartier appetite, go for the classic BK Lounge Burger: simple, satisfying, and juicy. It's everything a burger should be.

Crawl over to the Ink Block for the last South End stop.

10

HEAD TO LION'S TAIL FOR THE BEST OF THE INK BLOCK

The Ink Block is one of the hot new sub neighborhoods in the South End. Filled with luxury apartment buildings and spin studios, it is a chic place to be. And the area finally has a neighborhood hangout: LION'S TAIL. Everything a neighborhood spot should be, Lion's Tail is perfect for a date night, a drink with friends, or a family dinner. The food is exciting, the drinks are fun, and in a cool, unfussy setting, you are going to leave happy.

The plates are set up for sharing, so don't be afraid to order a bunch of things for the table. You are going to want to hang out and shoot the breeze for a while.

The pork belly, octopus, hanger steak, and little neck clams are all worth the trip. Tasty and creative, you will instantly fall in love with Chef Pagano's seasonal menus like I have.

"We are all about simple, fresh, seasonal food with local ingredients and creative cocktails in a fun, casual environment."

– Chef Dan Pagano

Southie

Sunday Funday: From Broadway to Castle Island

SOUTH BOSTON—OR "SOUTHIE" AS WE BOSTONIANS SO LOV-INGLY REFER TO IT (and how all those bad accents referred to it in *The Departed*)—is one of the neighborhoods that has gone through a lot of change in the past few years. Once the bastion of the Irish mob and now a mecca of antique stores and high-end consignment shops, Southie has that eclectic mix of old and new found throughout Boston.

Since Southie is now home to more recent grads than probably any other neighborhood in Boston, it's no surprise that the food scene is filled with fun, tasty spots. But what will surprise you when you visit Southie is the level of variety that is available. You can get tacos and margaritas on the same day that you get a gourmet Italian meal. And on a nice summer day, you can get my go-to lobster roll while watching the boats go by in the harbor. Southie is no longer home to the mob; it's now home to some tasty meals! Let's get crawling!

THE SOUTHIE CRAWL

1. See the best that old Southie has to offer at SULLIVAN'S CASTLE ISLAND
   2080 WILLIAM J. DAY BLVD., SOUTH BOSTON, (617) 268-5685, SULLIVANSCASTLEISLAND.COM

2. See the best that new Southie has to offer at LOCO
   412 W. BROADWAY, BOSTON, (617) 917-5626, LOCOSOUTHBOSTON.COM

3. Experience Sunday Funday with the cool kids at LINCOLN TAVERN
   425 W. BROADWAY, SOUTH BOSTON, (617) 765-8636, LINCOLNSOUTHBOSTON.COM

4. Recuperate from Sunday Funday and soak it all up with some Bolognese at CAPO
   443 W. BROADWAY, SOUTH BOSTON, (617) 993-8080, CAPOSOUTHBOSTON.COM

5. Start your own Sunday Funday at the other end of the world at WORDEN HALL
   22 W. BROADWAY, BOSTON, (617) 752-4206, WORDENHALL.COM

6. Hang out with 200 of your closest friends any weekend afternoon at COPPERSMITH
   40 W. 3RD ST., SOUTH BOSTON, (617) 658-3452, COPPERSMITHBOSTON.COM

7. Yes, they now do cheese plates in Southie, try one at FROMAGE
   401 W. BROADWAY, (617) 464-4300, (617) 347-2272, FROMAGEBOSTON.COM

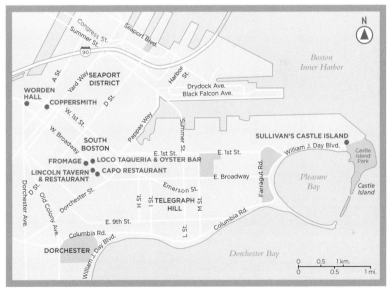

LET'S HEAD TO SOUTHIE!

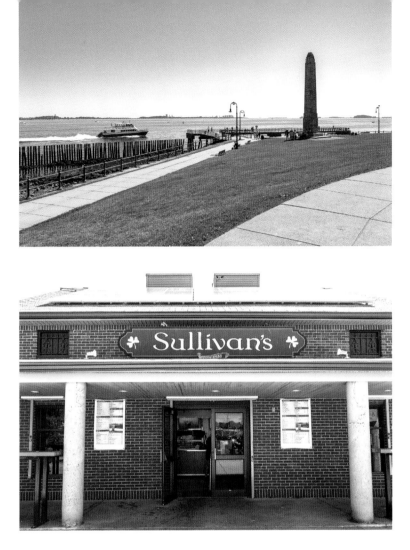

SEE THE BEST THAT OLD SOUTHIE HAS TO OFFER AT SULLIVAN'S CASTLE ISLAND

Like I said, Southie has changed, and I think it's safe to say that we are officially in the era of "new Southie." Just 5 years ago if I told someone I was going to Southie, they would definitely have asked "Why?" and then added, "Be home before dark."

But now that conversation has turned into: "Oh do you go to yoga on Broadway too? Let's do brunch afterwards!" And while I'm about to share my love of all these new wonderful brunch spots with you, I just have to start this chapter off with the real OG: SULLIVAN'S CASTLE ISLAND (or Sully's as anyone in Boston calls it).

As its name suggests, Sully's is located on Castle Island, which is found all the way at the eastern end of Southie and is not, in fact, an island at all but rather a peninsula. It's also the site of an old military base called Fort Independence, which has been the location of various fortifications since the 1600s. And today, Castle Island is right near the Southie beaches and has a beautiful view of the harbor and the planes leaving Logan. This is a popular area for Southie families to walk dogs or push baby strollers on sunny Sunday mornings.

Castle Island is beautiful, with views of Boston Harbor and plenty of benches to relax on and take it all in. It makes so much sense that Sully's has been a favorite since it opened in 1951. The only eating establishment on the "island," Sully's serves perfect picnic fare (think hot dogs, hamburgers, and lobster rolls). And for drinks the lime rickeys and smoothies are your best bets.

On a beautiful sunny day, there is nothing better than grabbing one of Sully's well-valued lobster rolls (during the summer of 2017, they were only $14.95) and taking a stroll around the fort before picking a bench from which to watch the boats go by in the harbor. And I have to note that while Sully's is technically a "hot dog joint" (and one of the last remaining such joints in the Boston area, I might add), they take their food and drink very seriously. The quality is exactly what you'd want: clean, reliable, and well priced. The box of fried clams doesn't disappoint, and the hotdogs are a delightful throwback. I mean seriously, when was the last time, outside of a baseball game, that you sat in the open air and ate a hotdog? Think about it, and if it's been a while go to Sully's!

And afterwards, why not try something new in Southie, the fabulous tacos at Loco!

2

SEE THE BEST THAT NEW SOUTHIE HAS TO OFFER AT LOCO

I think **LOCO** is the perfect example of the dramatic change Southie has gone through. Never in a million years would my father have thought that there would be a trendy taco bar on the same street that Whitey Bulger used to control. And yet look at where we are today! Loco serves some of my favorite tacos and margaritas in town and offers live music several days a week.

The live music, flavorful tacos, and creative margaritas make it easy to see why Loco is now a local favorite. With 7 different margaritas to choose from and 10 tacos on the menu at any one time, this place is definitely a crowd pleaser.

Loco is located on the ubiquitous Broadway Street, which has always

been the hub of Southie and is now the hub of all the fun, boozy brunch locales that recent college grads will be enjoying for years to come. Seriously, Southie has to be the most popular neighborhood for recent graduates. If you walk down Broadway on a weekend afternoon in October, you will be swarmed by boys in Patagonia vests and girls carrying yoga mats. It's certainly a new world for the longtime residents still sticking it out!

A funky taco bar is exactly what the area needed, and the fun, tasty menu certainly delivers. Whether you go with the fish, steak, chicken, or other amazing creations on the menu, you'll leave satisfied (especially when you wash it all down with the coconut margarita).

To keep the day going, why not pretend you're a Southie cool kid and head to Lincoln?

"The rise of South Boston's West Side seemed inevitable back in 2012 when we opened Lincoln Tavern, although the retail profile in the neighborhood certainly didn't reflect that. Lincoln Tavern was developed as a catch-all bridge concept that served the needs of a uniquely diverse neighborhood in its early stages of gentrification. Lincoln served as the gathering place for both lifelong residents and a new young professional demographic moving into new developments.

Over the past 5 years, the pace of gentrification in South Boston's West Side has moved at light speed, and we focused on developing an elevated food scene to meet the needs of our new residential community. From there, we have developed Loco and Capo to provide accessible Mexican and Italian to the community, and now Asian food options. Development and the amenities that support them, like restaurants, have completely changed the landscape of South Boston's west side."

— *Eric Aulenback, owner of Lincoln Tavern,
Loco Taqueria, Capo Restaurant, and Fat Baby*

3

EXPERIENCE SUNDAY FUNDAY WITH THE COOL KIDS AT LINCOLN TAVERN

Any 25-year-old who has lived in Southie for more than a day will tell you that the most Southie thing to do is Sunday Funday. While for many cities across America this is not a new concept, for Boston it's revolutionary. With so many brunch spots within proximity—i.e. all within walking distance from one another on Broadway Street—Southie is now the day-long Sunday marathon drinking hub of Boston. And at the center of the whole scene is LINCOLN TAVERN. With its wide façade on Broadway, its playful brunch dishes entice people to come in, and the lively atmosphere gets them to linger for most of the day.

Lincoln has that fun, "bro-y," fantasy football vibe that has something for everyone. If you want to be in the throes of it all, post up at the bar. And if you want to hear your dining companions speak, nab a spot near the giant windows.

The brunch dishes include things like Fruity Pebble Pancakes and French toast. The pancakes are fluffy and creamy, and the French toast is thick and comes with a giant scoop of vanilla ice cream. What more could you ask for? Well except maybe a Classic Bloody Mary, which they also happen to do really well!

Oh and did I mention that they are now doing brunch every day of the week? If you didn't go to Lincoln did you even go to Southie?

4

RECUPERATE FROM SUNDAY FUNDAY AND SOAK IT ALL UP WITH SOME BOLOGNESE AT CAPO

The problem with Sunday Funday is that you are usually starting all the fun before noon, which for most people means that you are struggling by dinnertime. So to balance out the day, be sure to grab a reservation at **CAPO**, Lincoln's sister restaurant next door, for a dinner of heartwarming Bolognese and ravioli.

With spectacular charcuterie, pasta, and entrees, Capo is a delightful Italian surprise in an old Irish world. It boasts a solid wine-by-the-glass list, as well. If you aren't up for the trek to the North End, Capo can fill all your red sauce cravings. And it shares many of the same social benefits as Lincoln: the view onto Broadway, a fun crowd, and a great bar menu if you aren't in the mood for a full sit-down dinner.

Winning dishes include the Beet Ravioli, Steak Tartare, Chicken Cacciatore, and Rigatoni Bolognese. Oh and the desserts aren't bad either!

Sunday Funday never has to end in Southie. Next, try Wordon Hall, which is still a hidden gem!

 START YOUR OWN SUNDAY FUNDAY
AT THE OTHER END OF THE WORLD
AT WORDEN HALL

Most people going to Southie for dinner or a night out are thinking of the Lincoln/Capo part of Broadway Street, yet way up toward the Broadway T stop is **WORDEN HALL**. Probably the most underrated Southie spot, Worden Hall has an excellently creative brunch program, food and drinks both. Also, the staff is excellent. Thoughtful, attentive, helpful service can truly take a dining experience to the next level, and that combined with the innovative dishes will keep you coming back again and again.

The Crispy Polenta Fries and Country-Fried Steak and Eggs are great dishes to start with at Worden Hall. Paired with some fabulously cheap mimosas, you can't go wrong. I'm calling it right now: once word gets out about these $4 mimosas, Worden Hall could easily be this year's Lincoln. So head on over while you can!

But seriously, their brunch cocktail game is on point. The mimosas are one thing, but if you need more of a pick me up, go for the Sgt. Reckless, a play on an iced Irish coffee.

And if you're feeling like a hearty meal to start off the day, the Deep-Dish Pizza and Worden Breakfast are the plates for you!

I see Worden Hall as being even more of a destination for Bostonians who don't live in Southie. With its proximity to the Broadway T stop,

Worden Hall should be swimming with Back Bayers wanting to dip their toes into the beast that has become Broadway Street. I sometimes find myself staying away from Southie because of its seemingly inconvenient distance from downtown, yet I could easily jump on the Red Line from Downtown Crossing to get to Wordan Hall in just a few minutes—and so could you!

Next up on our food crawl of Southie is Coppersmith.

Sgt. Reckless Recipe

4 parts Cold Brew Espresso
1 part espresso-infused
Four Roses bourbon
Heavy dash of vanilla
    simple syrup
Milk to taste

Shake all ingredients
together with ice until cold,
then pour over fresh ice in
tall glass.

6

HANG OUT WITH 200 OF YOUR CLOSEST FRIENDS ANY WEEKEND AFTERNOON AT COPPERSMITH

COPPERSMITH is the place for a party. With a roof deck and a warehouse-like open layout in the main dining room, this is where you can come with 10 or 15 people and never feel like you're imposing. With a spacious bar and plenty of high-top seating, this is the spot for casual drinks and apps. With fun cocktail creations, such as the Berry Cooler and the Blue-Haired Lady, Coppersmith is a relatively fresh newcomer to the ever-growing and changing food scene in this part of the city. And if you make it in for brunch, they have an elaborate make-your-own Bloody Mary Bar that is worth checking out as well.

On the food side of things, the classics are the winners. Try the Chicken and Waffles or the Glazed Chicken Wings.

And it is worth mentioning that their large roof deck is open during the warmer months.

7 YES, THEY NOW DO CHEESE PLATES IN SOUTHIE, TRY ONE AT FROMAGE

A well-developed food scene usually means that there are some unexpected winners around every corner. Southie used to be a haven of Irish pubs and sports bars, and while it still has its fair share of these (and we like it that way), you can now get a decent cheese plate in the neighborhood too! **FROMAGE** is the neighborhood wine bar that Southie never knew it needed.

The highlight here is definitely the cheese and charcuterie selection. The cheese plates come with all the accoutrements: jam, mustard, cornichons, grapes, strawberries, and some lovely toast and crackers. Pair that with a glass of wine and you've got a nice afternoon ahead of you!

Downtown

On Saturday's We Wear Louboutin and Drink Craft Cocktails

BOSTON DOESN'T REALLY HAVE A WELL-DEFINED DOWNTOWN, but the area generally includes Downtown Crossing, the Leather District, and the Financial District. As a resident of said Downtown, I can say that the neighborhood is now a destination rather than just somewhere you commute to Monday through Friday. And falafel, dumplings, sushi, and charcuterie are all some of the reasons people are coming to Downtown! With so many new hot spots, Downtown is another neighborhood that has morphed greatly from what it was just a few years ago. No longer is the area just filled with lunchtime spots (not to say that I don't love all the Downtown lunchtime spots!) and bars filled with the after-work crowd. The new Downtown has innovative eateries, stylish cocktail bars and restaurants fit for foodies. From restaurants like O Ya that have pumped out some fabulous young chefs (looking at you Tracy!) to newcomers like Ruka that are setting the tone for the zip code, Downtown is definitely worthy of a visit.

THE DOWNTOWN CRAWL

1. **Grab some flaming waygu at RUKA**
   505 WASHINGTON ST., BOSTON, (617) 266-0102, RUKARESTOBAR.COM

2. **Put on your Loubs for a classy night out at PABU**
   3 FRANKLIN ST., BOSTON, (857) 327-7228, MICHAELMINA.NET/
   RESTAURANTS/BOSTON/PABU-BOSTON

3. **Grab the gals for a couple glasses of wine at HALEY.HENRY**
   45 PROVINCE ST., BOSTON, (617) 208-6000, HALEYHENRY.COM

4. **Celebrate something special with the Omakase at O YA**
   9 EAST ST., BOSTON, (617) 654-9900, O-YA.RESTAURANT

5. **Beat sad desk lunch syndrome with a giant pastrami creation from SAM LAGRASSA'S**
   44 PROVIDENCE ST., BOSTON, (617) 357-6861, SAMLAGRASSAS.COM

6. **Live like a FALAFEL KING**
   260 WASHINGTON ST., BOSTON, (617) 227-6400, FALAFELKINGBOSTON.COM

7. **Cultivate a taste for charcuterie at CULTIVAR**
   1 COURT ST., BOSTON, (617) 979-8203, CULTIVARBOSTON.COM

8. **Brunch at TRADE**
   540 ATLANTIC AVE., BOSTON, (617) 451-1234, TRADE-BOSTON.COM

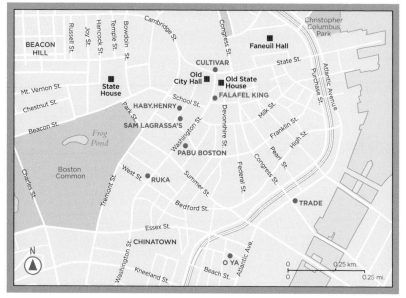

LET'S HEAD DOWNTOWN!

1

GRAB SOME FLAMING WAYGU AT RUKA

Located on the ground floor of the brand-new Godfrey Hotel, **RUKA RESTOBAR** is very of-the-moment. Asian fusion has taken Boston by storm, and Ruka is one of my new favorites. With maki rolls featuring roasted waygu and all the Pisco you could ever ask for, Ruka is a hip, fun Downtown spot.

Come for the drinks and the atmosphere but stay for the food. The bar is cool and the drinks are tasty and creative, but don't forget to eat. The menu is made for sharing, so pick a few plates for the table and linger as long as you wish.

With a dark, mysterious tiki bar vibe, Ruka is the place for a romantic night out with your new fling or the one who already has your heart. Either way, you're in for a steamy evening.

To continue the Asian fusion fun, you need to head to Pabu, just off Washington Street at 1 Franklin.

2

PUT ON YOUR LOUBS FOR A CLASSY NIGHT OUT AT PABU

The other big Asian fusion destination that has popped up down-town is **PABU** by Michael Mina. Located on the second floor of Millennium Tower, Pabu has all the makings of a hit. An exclusive location, a smart menu, a chic atmosphere—all the things that stylish Bostonians should fall in love with!

Whether you come in for lunch or dinner, you will not be disappointed. The servers are thoughtful and knowledgeable. Everything from the udon to the sushi is immaculately prepared, and the view of bustling Franklin Street is just delightful.

Perfect maki paired with a champagne cocktail is the way all lunches were meant to be. Reclaim your ladies-who-lunch status at Pabu, the fusion spot with a view.

After you've lunched, continue your culture fest with some wine and tinned fish at haley.henry.

 GRAB THE GALS FOR A COUPLE GLASSES OF WINE AT HALEY.HENRY

The vibe downtown is funky. With the influx of high-end condos and apartment buildings, the demand for cool, unexpected eateries is clearly on the rise. Never in "old" Boston would Asian fusion and a Spanish tinned fish–focused wine bar be neighbors. Yet that's exactly what this brave new world looks like.

HALEY.HENRY takes up a slice of Province Street and is doing its best to fill it with sardines and rare wines.

> "Tinned fish has always been shoved onto the back burner in terms of American cuisine. We've taken a great deal of time to curate the 'best of the best' from around the world, so naturally, its time for these little gems to shine."
>
> – *Haley Fortier, restaurateur*

Pop in to grab a bite at the bar and a glass of something from a vineyard far, far away. The vision of restaurateur Haley Fortier is very forward thinking. Inspired by her travels, Haley has brought all the gems of the European countryside to our little Downtown. Thanks Haley!

After enjoying simple pleasures, go for the more complicated ones and make a night of it at O Ya.

4 CELEBRATE SOMETHING SPECIAL WITH THE OMAKASE AT O YA

Consistently at the top of all the restaurant guides since opening, O YA should be on every foodie's bucket list. Specializing in precision, O Ya offers up some amazing ingredients prepared in the most meticulous manner you'll find anywhere in town.

While I highly recommend stopping into O Ya for any occasion, if you have something special to celebrate, their Omakase menu is the way to go. Trust me, it is a treat! Beginning with the Kumamoto Oyster, this grand tasting menu is truly a culinary journey that every foodie must experience at least once in his or her life.

As you move through each course, each dish amazes more than the last. The flavors won't be found on any other menu in Boston. Where else are you going to see Vietnamese Dashi Caramel? Seriously, O Ya is something spe-

cial. And when you do stop in, try to snag a seat at the chef's counter and watch in amazement as each plate is meticulously prepared.

O Ya is the kind of place that is a little intimidating even to the seasoned diner, but don't worry, the staff is extremely helpful in aiding your menu navigation. If you are going à la carte, you should really be ordering 10 to 15 items for a party of 2 or 3. And don't neglect the drink menu either. A nice sake or glass of wine will up the impact on the taste buds, so ask for some advice there as well.

Tucked around the corner off South Street, on East Street, O Ya is the original cool kid's Downtown hangout. With just a small sign marking the door, you feel as if you are sneaking into a secret supper club headed by master sushi chefs. So "Ya," it's worth it!

While O Ya is the place for a lovely dinner, lunch doesn't have to be any less exciting. Excite the taste buds at Sam LaGrassa's.

5

BEAT SAD DESK LUNCH SYNDROME WITH A GIANT PASTRAMI CREATION FROM SAM LAGRASSA'S

Downtown Boston is obviously filled with thousands of offices, which means thousands of hungry office workers come lunchtime. While many of us subject ourselves to sad desk lunches most days of the week, either in the name of laziness, frugality, or anti-socialness, when you do feel like venturing out into the wild for a tasty lunch, one that is worth the calories is **SAM LAGRASSA'S**.

Located on Province Street, close to Downtown Crossing and the Financial District, Sam LaGrassa's is the quintessential urban lunch deli. The winners here are the gigantic sandwiches, piled high with pastrami and oozy, gooey sauce. My favorite is the Chipotle Pastrami, but the Jumbo Reuben and the Famous Rumanian Pastrami are also top picks.

I think you deserve a fair warning, though: these sandwiches are not messing around. They could easily be your lunch *and* dinner. So don't be a hero. Eat half now and save the other half for later. And be sure to grab plenty of napkins because these things aren't exactly dainty. Roll up your sleeves and get in there (especially if you go with my fav, the Chipotle Pastrami; it's juicy for better or worse!).

6 LIVE LIKE A FALAFEL KING

Another of my favorite homegrown lunch spots is **FALAFEL KING**. I used to go to the Falafel King that was located behind a convenience store on a sketchier part of Winter Street. In the past few years they have flourished and now have a flagship location on the corner of Summer and Otis Streets. They also have another satellite location in the area.

Falafel King will satisfy all your falafel, chicken, and rice needs. I like to go for the Classic Falafel Salad or the Chicken Swarma Plate. Oh and here's a pro tip: instead of trying to stuff the falafel they give to you in line down your throat while you're trying to order and pay, just save it until they hand you your box of food and throw it in there. You've just increased your falafel count by 30 percent!

The crispy falafel, tangy salad, and creamy hummus are just the things you need to fuel even your busiest of days. So head on over to the King and grab some grub!

Stay in the Mediterranean and head to Cultivar for some fantastic mezze and charcuterie plates.

7

CULTIVATE A TASTE FOR CHARCUTERIE AT CULTIVAR

Another newcomer to the scene, **CULTIVAR** is the new restaurant located in the trendy Ames Hotel on State Street. It certainly has cultivated a sense of intrigue due to its location, chic interior, and fun menu. The perfect spot to grab a bite after work or a drink with a friend, Cultivar is the kind of place where you just want to sip a tasty drink and snack on charcuterie. Good thing they do a mean charcuterie board!

With several types of cured meats and cheeses to choose from, this is what a charcuterie board should look like. But what pleasantly surprised me the last time I was there was the dessert. The pastry chef is creative, smart, and seriously good at plating. These desserts could fit in on any fine-dining menu in town. Definitely don't skip dessert when you stop by for that drink. Oh and in the summer months, they have a lovely patio that is perfect for enjoying a wonderfully fresh seafood tower!

Cultivar is light and airy both inside and out, with a menu to match. I stopped in when I wanted to try something new, and I can see it quickly becoming a new neighborhood hangout.

8 BRUNCH AT TRADE

Speaking of neighborhood hangouts, Jody Adams is another one of those Boston culinary behemoths capable of turning a spot into a destination. TRADE, which opened in 2011, has been a hit all these years. With Jody's Mediterranean-inspired cuisine, Trade is a buzzing spot after work each night and during boozy brunch on the weekends.

All of the fresh options pair well with the delicious cocktails coming out of the bar. Start with some tartare and then move on to the avocado toast. And if your appetite can handle it, go for the Trade Burger and fries. Sometimes a juicy burger is just what the doctor ordered, so head to Trade to satisfy that craving. Then wash it all down with their signature cocktail, Beets by Trade.

Located on the edge of the Financial District, on your way into the Seaport, Trade was a turning point for this part of Downtown. It gave us all somewhere to go after work but also a place we could see ourselves making the hike to on weekends. Trade has certainly brought in a lot of energy and flavor to the neighborhood.

Beets by Trade Recipe

Shake with ice till chilled:

1.5 oz Ketel One vodka
1 oz beet syrup
.75 lolita mix (pineapple,
    lime, agave)

Serve in Collins glass and
top with crushed ice and a
mint sprig garnish.

Chinatown

Dumplings (and More)
Worth the Line Out the Door

CHINATOWN HAS ALWAYS BEEN MY FAVORITE NEIGHBORHOOD FOR FOOD. Honestly, there is no going wrong here. For some reason, though, many Bostonians are scared away by the "intimidating" menus. Boston has one of the best Chinatowns in the country; it's a bastion for delicious, diverse, and modern Asian cuisines. From old classics to trendy newcomers, Chinatown's food scene is expansive. There are the Insta-worthy creations and authentic dishes, that make the food worth the occasional line down the street. Yes, many of the best restaurants in Chinatown don't take reservations and can get busy at dinnertime. Trust me, though, the wait is worth it. It would take a lifetime to really explore all the nooks and crannies in the neighborhood, so you better get cracking! Any chance I get, I try a new dish or a new restaurant and so should you! But be warned, there are new hotspots cropping up all the time, so I hope you're hungry! As someone who has been coming here to eat since I was a little girl, Chinatown will always be the closest to my heart. RIP Chau Chows.

THE CHINATOWN CRAWL

1. **The first stop for anyone visiting Chinatown has to be**
    GOURMET DUMPLING HOUSE
    52 BEACH ST., BOSTON, (617) 338-6223, GOURMETDUMPLINGHOUSE.COM

2. **Bring your Insta-famous friends to the new hot spot, DOUBLE CHIN**
    86 HARRISON AVE., BOSTON, (617) 482-0682, DOUBLECHINBOS.COM

3. **Grab dim sum the next day at BUBOR CHA CHA**
    45 BEACH ST., BOSTON, (617) 482-3338, BUBORCHACHA.COM

4. **Head to SHOJO for a drink after work**
    9 TYLER ST., BOSTON, (617) 423-7888, SHOJOBOSTON.COM

5. **Dine at BLR for the clash of the new and old**
    13 HUDSON ST., BOSTON, (617) 338-4988, BLRBYSHOJO.COM

6. **Can't decide between hot or cold? The Q is the answer**
    660 WASHINGTON ST., BOSTON, (857) 350-3968, THEQUSA.COM

7. **Head to PEACH FARM for some late night indulgences**
    4 TYLER ST., BOSTON, (617) 482-1116, PEACHFARM.NET

8. **Warm your heart at PHO PASTEUR**
    628 WASHINGTON ST., BOSTON, (617) 482-7467, PHOPASTEURBOSTON.NET

9. **Satisfy your cravings at CRAVE-MAD FOR CHICKEN**
    75 KNEELAND ST., BOSTON, (617) 338-0188, CRAVEMADFORCHICKEN.COM

10. **Order the Peking Duck at CHINA PEARL**
    9 TYLER ST., BOSTON, (617) 426-4338, CHINAPEARLBOSTON.COM

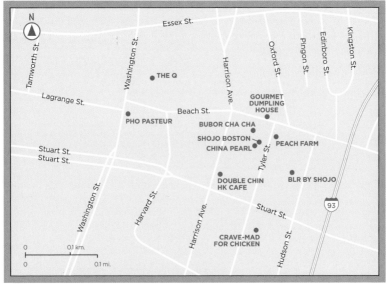

LET'S HEAD TO CHINATOWN!

1

THE FIRST STOP FOR ANYONE VISITING CHINATOWN HAS TO BE GOURMET DUMPLING HOUSE

GOURMET DUMPLING HOUSE is everything you want from Chinatown: a line out the door, juicy dumplings, and hot tea. Nothing more, nothing less. Seriously, if I could have only one more meal in Boston, I have to say that this would be it. Start with some mini juicy dumplings, then move to the Taiwanese-style rice cake with pork and veggies, and finish with the house specialty, the sautéed watercress. It's a match made in heaven.

If you've never been, here is the insider's way to eat the mini juicy dumplings (aka soup dumplings): put one in a soup spoon, hold the spoon in your left hand and chopsticks in right hand, use the chopsticks to grasp the dumpling from the spoon, bite a tiny hole in the side of the dumpling, suck a little bit of that amazing juice out of it, and then swallow it all down.

For the entirety of my time in Boston I've lived within a 10-minute walk from Beach Street, and during the horrific blizzard of 2015, I trudged all the way to the only open restaurant during the storm: Gourmet Dumpling House. Open consistently during the snow days, we fed our cold souls with all the wonderful things from that small kitchen. Food can really cure all, and in the middle of a miserable winter, sometimes warm dumplings and hot vegetables are all you need to soothe the pain. Thank you Gourmet Dumpling House for making all the problems of the world go away with your delicious food. So if you are ever walking by and see a long line and wonder if it's worth it, always remember that yes, yes it is.

2 BRING YOUR INSTA-FAMOUS FRIENDS TO THE NEW HOT SPOT, DOUBLE CHIN

While Gourmet Dumpling House is a tough act to follow, my friend Gloria Chin and her wonderful staff do a terrific job of it at **DOUBLE CHIN**. Taking a whole new look at what a Chinatown restaurant should be, Gloria has taken things to the next level. With offerings like Cube Toast and Capri Fun on the menu, Double Chin is the Chinatown for the new generation. With fun plays on traditional food and new and exciting fusions, Double Chin always promises a good time.

Gloria has clearly figured out the recipe for appealing to the Millennial crowd because every night the restaurant is filled to the brim with 20-somethings laughing with their friends.

Bring all your friends and split the watermelon bomber and a few savory bites. And of course you need to finish the evening off with a Cube Toast, which is at the same time the most ridiculous and amazing dessert you will ever have. Seriously, it's totally worth the trip to Chinatown! If you've had enough new-fangled bites, the next stop, Bubor Cha Cha will satisfy the classic cravings!

"My vision for Double Chin was to create a restaurant that truly embodied my identity. I am a native Bostonian who grew up in a Chinese household—that's why our menu offers glorified American classics with modern Asian twists. My inspiration for the Cube Toast was to create a crazy over-the-top dessert that combined different temperatures, textures, and flavor profiles. It is like the wicked fun love child of a French toast and ice cream sundae on steroids! I wanted there to be a social aspect to the dessert too—it's like a rated G version of a scorpion bowl that no one can resist Instagramming."

– Gloria Chin, restaurateur

ANATOMY OF A CUBE TOAST:

- The toast, baked in a square mold and then hollowed out.

- The ice cream, matcha or chocolate always available plus seasonal flavors.

- Pocky sticks, because they are delicious.

- Fruit, candy and cereal, because why not!

3

GRAB DIM SUM THE NEXT DAY AT BUBOR CHA CHA

The Chinese figured out this whole brunch thing about 1,000 years before the rest of us. Dim sum is the amazing Chinese small-plate brunch of your dreams. And Boston's Chinatown has some fantastic spots to grab dim sum. **BUBOR CHA CHA** on Beach Street is unique in that it offers its dim sum menu all day, everyday, not just on weekends.

There are so many tasty things that will come your way. From giant shumai to several varieties of shrimp dumplings to fried chicken feet, you will leave fat and happy for sure! Seriously, don't be afraid to order 10 or 15 plates to share with your friends and family. Dim sum is a time to come together over tasty morsels and to get ready for the rest of the day (or night since, like I said, Bubor Cha Cha offers dim sum all day, everyday!).

Next up is a hip spot perfect for some happy hour drinks, Shojo.

4 HEAD TO SHOJO FOR A DRINK AFTER WORK

SHOJO, while owned by the same people who own one of the Chinatown classics, China Pearl, is part of the new wave of Asian fusion spots in the neighborhood. Staying true to the heritage of the area, but also speaking to the younger generation, Shojo is a funky reinvention of Chinatown. With things like chicken and waffles and several varieties of bao, as well as a killer drink menu, Shojo is a place to hang out after work as well as the place to get the night started.

And their lunch menu is a great way to recover the next day. As soon as you walk in and see the classic kung fu movies playing on the TV and the gigantic wall mural, you'll know you're in the right place. And when you see a plate of food go by, you'll want to stick around for sure.

If you feel like checking out another Chinatown gem, why not head around the corner to BLR, which is also by the same folks as Shojo.

DINE AT BLR FOR THE CLASH OF THE NEW AND OLD

You just know a place called Best Little Restaurant is going to be amazing. And the revamped iteration, **BLR BY SHOJO**, is even better. BLR is a tiny subterranean sliver of a restaurant located on Hudson Street.

With a menu that is equally as lean and mean, this little restaurant is definitely punching above its weight class. When things like Roasted Bone Marrow and the Best Little Trout arrive at your table, you'll immediate know that you aren't at your run-of-the-mill Chinese restaurant. BLR is an amalgamation of the best of the old and new. And it is a breath of fresh air.

It is funky, cool, and dark, but the menu is bright and delicious.

You'll be eating the Salt and Pepper Smelts like potato chips before you even realize it. Dipped in a little bit of aioli, they are addicting. Oh and don't skip the cold apps; there are some winners on there as well. The Fu-Yu Cucumber Salad is particularly refreshing and crunchy.

Pair any of these all-star dishes with some sake and you and your crew are in for a fun night.

Next up, the Q, is where you'll want to be this winter. When the wind is blowing, you'll be cozy inside with some hotpot.

6 CAN'T DECIDE BETWEEN HOT OR COLD? THE Q IS THE ANSWER

You know those days when you want something both cozy and crisp at the same time and you just can't put your finger on what you could go for? Well, the Q has the answer for you: Mongolian Hot Pot with a side of sushi.

Traditionally speaking, **Q RESTAURANT** is a hot pot joint, but its vast menu has some other winners on there too. Start with some creative sushi rolls and then move into the exciting world of the hot pot.

The preparation of the sushi and sashimi is immaculate, and the fish is so fresh, it will pass any sushi aficionado's test. I mean, look at them, they are just gorg!

And if you are in the mood for something lighter, one of the crazy sushi rolls paired with a fun tropical cocktail makes for a nice snack or light dinner.

But if you are looking for a feast, Q has you covered as well. A hot pot can be pretty much whatever you want it to be. From seafood to chicken to beef to pork to veggies, they've got it all. So take a look at the menu or ask the server for recommendations because there are so many tasty treats available. And when it comes to the broth, you have to go half spicy, half regular to try both ends of the spectrum!

Chinatown has something for everyone, and also something for all times of the day. If you happen to find yourself in the neighborhood late at night, our next stop if the place for you!

7 HEAD TO PEACH FARM FOR SOME LATE NIGHT INDULGENCES

For better or worse, many Bostonians come to Chinatown on their way home from one of the nearby nightclubs since the neighborhood is home to most of the few-late night eateries available in Boston. And there's just something about low mein at 3:00 a.m. that hits the spot.

One of these hot spots for both late night revelers and industry pros is PEACH FARM. It's a traditional Boston Chinatown establishment in every sense of the word, with pink tablecloths, speedy service, and family-style dishes included.

Come here with an appetite because, with generous portions and friendly prices, Peach Farm deserves your attention, whether it's 7:00 p.m. or 2:00 a.m. No matter what time you show up, you're going to be greeted with an amazing menu, and you'll definitely leave with a full belly.

You can never have enough Pho, so of course Pho Pasteur made the list. Read on to learn about this delicious Vietnamese spot.

8 WARM YOUR HEART AT PHO PASTEUR

Chinatown is home to a diverse Asian community, and that includes a vibrant Vietnamese population. So we are lucky to have a few very popular pho spots. My go-to is **PHO PASTEUR**.

When I'm in the mood for bun or pho, this is where I head.

Bun is a delightful bowl filled with vermicelli noodles, veggies, and your choice of meats, all tied together with fresh spices and a tangy sauce.

Whether it's the middle of the summer or the dead of winter, Pho Pasteur has something that will cure whatever is ailing you. If there's a foot of snow outside, go for some pho, and if it's 90 degrees out, a light bowl of bun will do the trick.

Anyone craving Korean fried chicken in Chinatown is in luck—our next stop is the place to go.

SATISFY YOUR CRAVINGS AT CRAVE-MAD FOR CHICKEN

Downtown Boston, I hate to say it, has a lack of good Korean places, but **CRAVE-MAD FOR CHICKEN** is doing its best to hold down the fort. Known for its Korean-style chicken, Crave offers a wide range of tasty things with Korean flare. However, my consistent order is Beef Bulgogi, Seafood Jigae, and the Angry Chicken.

The Bulgogi and Jigae are prepared exactly as they should be. And the Angry Chicken will cure any craving for spicy fried chicken you have for a month. Seriously, this stuff is so good, you'll eat way too much of it and swear you are never eating again. Of course that lasts only until the next time someone says, "fried chicken." Then you immediately think of Crave.

But like my other go-to, Q Restaurant, Crave has some solid sushi, too. With beautiful rolls and fresh sashimi, if you're looking for the lighter side of things, you won't be disappointed.

Our last stop on the Chinatown Crawl is one of the old standbys in the neighborhood and it is not to be missed.

10

ORDER THE PEKING DUCK AT CHINA PEARL

One of the matrons of Chinatown, **CHINA PEARL** is a grand old girl. With a menu steeped in both the classics and newer favorites, China Pearl offers you the full Chinatown experience. From dim sum to lunch to late night bites, you will find what you're looking for here. But to really experience the best China Pearl has to offer, you need to go big or go home.

The Peking Duck is the specialty. And boy do they do it right! Coursed out, you get to enjoy all of the duck. First comes the crispy skin with some tender meat. Then comes the soup and then more of the meat with noodles. Fit for a celebration, China Pearl's Peking Duck is something that any fan of Chinese cuisine needs to try the next time they are in Chinatown.

The North End

From There to Here, From Here to There, Pasta Is Still Everywhere!

FOREVER THE ORIGINAL "FOODIE" NEIGHBORHOOD, the North End knows what it's doing. It still holds true that if you are in the mood for a delicious Italian meal you should head to the North End. Ever since I was a little girl, the North End has been the place we'd go when there was something to celebrate. The Italians know how to have a good time and how to celebrate with food. From a family dinner, to a professional celebration, to a friend's birthday, the North End is always a crowd pleaser. Plan on plenty of pasta, cannoli and vino—you're in for a good time! Big flavors paired with big personalities is usually the hallmark of good Italian cooking, and in the North End, you'll see that for yourself. Fresh ingredients prepared with care is the name of the game out here. So whether you're in the mood for some pizza fit for royalty or some fresh veggies, the North End has got the good stuff!

THE NORTH END CRAWL

1. **Sit down for a family dinner at PAGLIUCA'S**
   14 PARMENTER ST., BOSTON, (617) 367-1504, PAGLIUCASRESTAURANT.COM

2. **Holy moly, MIKE'S cannolis!**
   300 HANIVER ST., BOSTON, (617) 742-3050, MIKESPASTRY.COM

3. **MAMMA MARIA knows best**
   3 N. SQUARE BOSTON, (617) 523-0077, MAMMAMARIA.COM

4. **The pizza you grew up with—yes, I'm talking about REGINA PIZZERIA**
   11½ THACHER ST., BOSTON, (617) 227-0765, PIZZERIAREGINA.COM

5. **Enjoy the afternoon with a latte like an Italian at CAFFE VITTORIA**
   290–296 HANOVER ST., BOSTON, (617) 227-7606, CAFFEVITTORIA.COM

6. **That dollar slice is nice at GALLERIA UMBERTO**
   289 HANOVER ST., BOSTON, (617) 227-5709

7. **Pick up some fresh veggies at HAYMARKET**
   CONGRESS & NEW SUDBURY STS., BOSTON, (617) 635-4500,
   HAYMARKETBOSTON.ORG

8. **Snack on some fruits de mer at IL MOLO**
   326 COMMERCIAL ST., BOSTON, (857) 277-1895, ILMOLOBOSTON.COM

9. **Head down the rabbit hole at STANZA DEI SIGARI**
   292 HANOVER ST., BOSTON, (617) 227-0295, STANZADEISIGARI.COM

10. **Escape to Sicily at CARMELINA'S**
    307 HANOVER ST., BOSTON, (617) 742-0020, CARMELINASBOSTON.COM

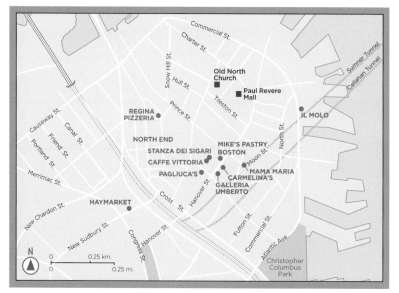

LET'S HEAD TO HANOVER STREET AND START
OUR NORTH END CRAWL! MANGIA!

1

SIT DOWN FOR A FAMILY DINNER AT PAGLIUCA'S

When you want a good, hearty meal, **PAGLIUCA'S** is the place to go. Whether you want lasagna, minestrone, or some eggplant parmesan, Pagliuca's has the Italian American classics and does them well.

There is something so heartwarming about a hot slice of lasagna in a cozy brick-walled dining room. And that combined with the buzzing atmosphere of the North End, which you get to take all during the summer months because the windows open onto Parmenter Street, makes for a magical evening. Having lived in Italy for 4 months, I can say that the Italians take dinnertime seriously, and Pagliuca's stays true to that classic approach. Focus on your dining companions, your food, and nothing else. The world can wait.

Simplicity is at the heart of Italian cuisine; quality ingredients prepared in a straightforward manner are all you need. And the kitchen at Pagliuca's understands that. The best things in life are often the simplest. Speaking of the best things, after dinner head to Mike's Pastry for the best cannoli in town!

HOLY MOLY, MIKE'S CANNOLI!

I'm sorry Modern Pastry, but I am staunchly in the MIKE'S Pastry camp. The size, the quality of the filling, and the number of amazing options for flavors does it for me. And I have to say the number of flavors of cannoli is just so impressive that even I, a lifelong Bostonian, haven't tried them all. The reason is that the ones I've had are just so good, it's hard to give them up. But I can safely say that the hazelnut, classic (chocolate chip), chocolate mousse, pistachio, and Florentine are among my top favorites. (Yes, I know that isn't narrowing it down that much.) But seriously just go for it; buy a box and take a bite from a few before committing to a whole one.

The line is always crazy at Mike's, so don't be afraid to throw a few elbows to make your way to the front, but do keep in mind that it is cash only. So get a Jackson out of your wallet and hold it high as you push your way to the front of the line. Try to have your flavors picked out before you get there because, trust me, there will be plenty of anxious people waiting for their turn behind you. And by the way, while cannolis are definitely the star, Mike's has a whole lot more to offer. Cakes, pastries, cookies, gelato— they do it all extremely well. No matter what, once you try something from Mike's you'll understand why anyone walking down the street with one of those blue and white boxes has such a big smile on their face. Quite simply, they went to Mike's!

Oh and here is a pro tip: a box of the Italian butter cookies make wonderful hostess gifts if you're in a rush! Trust me, you will definitely get a repeat invite if you come to the party bearing a pound or two of those bad boys. Maintain your rep as best friend to have in Boston at our next stop; the place to impress out-of-towners in the North End is Mamma Maria, our next stop!

3 MAMMA MARIA KNOWS BEST

Consistently ranked as the fine-dining destination in the North End, **MAMMA MARIA** is the place to impress your Italian cuisine-loving date. Quiet, romantic, and delicious, Mamma Maria always delivers on the charm. When you walk in, you feel as if you are walking into an old New England town house that just happens to be owned by an aristocratic Italian. Unlike the spots on

the bustling Hanover Street, this restaurant is placed back off the tranquil North Square Park. And the fine-dining atmosphere is just perfect for this little corner of the neighborhood.

Get ready to enjoy the finer things at Mamma Maria.

Ingredients are king here. The owner, John McGee, takes pride in sourcing high-quality seasonal ingredients that the kitchen highlights in its masterpieces. Aren't those chanterelles just beuts?

Oh and the pastry game is on point, as well. Sometimes even the best restaurants let dessert take a back seat to savory, but not at Mamma Maria. The puff is always flaky, and the whipped cream is like a velvety blanket. The execution of the simple yet technical aspects of a dish can make all the difference.

One more fun fact that speaks to the care with which the menu has been put together at Mamma Maria is the all-Italian wine list. Check it out for yourself!

For the diner ready for something a bit more casual, Regina Pizzeria is the classic that you will never get tired of.

4 THE PIZZA YOU GREW UP WITH—YES, I'M TALKING ABOUT REGINA PIZZERIA

While the battle between Santarpio's and **REGINA PIZZERIA** continues to rage on, there is one thing that Regina has going for it: it is the pizza that anyone born in Massachusetts was raised on. With locations all over the place, Regina Pizzeria is instantly recognizable to any Massachusetts son or daughter. And that Giambotta hits all the right notes.

Whether you're scarfing it down after a late night at work or while studying for the bar, this pizza will take you home again. Oh and the pizzas are huge (your move, Santarpio's). And for anyone from Massachusetts who has yet to make the pilgrimage to the original location in the North End, you have to do it. It might be touristy, but I think we all owe the Pizza Queen at least that much.

And there is really never a bad time to grab a pie! Afterwards, grab an afternoon espresso at Caffe Vittoria!

5

ENJOY THE AFTERNOON WITH A LATTE LIKE AN ITALIAN AT CAFFE VITTORIA

The Italians excel in the finer things in life: fashion, cars, food, and above all coffee. If you have ever been to Italy, you most likely noticed one thing immediately: the speed at which they consume their coffee. Instead of an on-the-go staple, coffee is something to linger over and savor. And a little bit of that sense of calm is brought to us Bostonians at **CAFFE VITTORIA**.

So when your day is feeling just a bit hurried, head over to Caffe Vittoria to take a step back to ponder what is truly important (i.e. how many cannolis you should bring back with you since Caffe Vittoria is right next to Mike's or what flavor of gelato you are going to get).

Snag a seat by the window and take a minute to just enjoy the view of Hanover Street. We are so lucky to have beautiful streets like this in Boston, so we should all take a second to soak that in once in a while.

Another European delight that we are lucky to have in Boston is street-style pizza, the square Sicilian slices that Galleria Umberto serves up at lunchtime are simple and delicious.

6 THAT DOLLAR SLICE IS NICE AT GALLERIA UMBERTO

While it may not be only a dollar anymore, **GALLERIA UMBERTO** is one of the most affordable lunches in town. With its hefty Sicilian-style square slices priced at only $1.70 (in 2017), eating here is a no-brainer.

But you have to be strategic when you go to Umberto's. You want to miss the rush but go too late and they might be sold out. My recommendation is to go early or go home.

Pizza by the slice is always nice, but at Galleria Umberto it's more than nice. It's special.

And similar to the pizza at Galleria Umberto, our next stop, Haymarket is a simple joy that you just can't miss if you are in the neighborhood.

7 PICK UP SOME FRESH VEGGIES AT HAYMARKET

The original Boston outdoor market, after which the T stop is named, **HAYMARKET** is still a mainstay for Bostonians looking for affordable fresh produce.

With all the fruits and vegetables you could ask for, Haymarket is the spot to grab some great fresh ingredients for dinner.

The organized chaos that permeates any outdoor market is part of the fun. The negotiation, the cash changing hands, and the overall bustling close quarters makes it an exciting place to be. Instead of heading to the supermarket this week, check out Haymarket. It's right off the Orange or Green Line—you can't miss it. It's the Haymarket stop!

SNACK ON SOME FRUITS DE MER AT IL MOLO

The North End is filled with mom and pop red sauce spots that have been around for decades, and everyone has a favorite (mine is Pagliuca's). But there are a few newcomers that are breathing new life into the established food scene.

IL MOLO is a great example of what a fresh take on an old neighborhood can do. Literally meaning "the Pier," Il Molo is a seafood lover's dream. Focusing on all the treasures of the sea, the restaurant pays homage to the maritime heritage of Boston and its location on the water on Commercial Street.

Any visit to Il Molo must begin with a seafood tower. Served with oysters, clams, lobster, shrimp, and the crudo of the day, it is the essence of the restaurant—fresh, tasty, and luxurious. This seafood tower was made for a hot day and a glass of crisp white wine.

Next I recommend heading to a few other cold apps. As you all must know by now, I'm a tartare aficionado, and I can safely say that the steak tartare at Il Molo is worth breaking from your all-seafood feast. But if you do want to stick to seafood, the lobster roll is also excellent. If you want something warm, the clam chowder would make any Bostonian proud. I particularly love the garnish; the fried clam adds something a little extra.

Il Molo is a cool spot to hang out with co-workers for happy hour. A few cocktails and a dozen oysters sounds like the perfect Friday afternoon to me! Afterwards, check out Stanza dei Sigari, an old world cigar lounge on Hanover Street.

9

HEAD DOWN THE RABBIT HOLE AT STANZA DEI SIGARI

The North End is filled with surprises and hidden gems. One such surprise is hidden in plain sight. Located at the front of Hanover Street, **STANZA DEI SIGARI** is a cigar bar from another era. You enter through a staircase decorated with vintage photos and posters, and when you arrive you are greeted with a subterranean lounge that is as mysterious as it sounds.

Filled with locals enjoying their cigars, it's nice to see that not all of old Boston has gone by the wayside. Even though I'm all about the new energy that has been coming to town, sometimes the old ways are just fine.

If you enjoy the occasional cigar, Stanza dei Sigari is a fine example of a casual cigar lounge with some Italian flair mixed in. After dinner, perhaps, head somewhere out of your normal routine and check it out for yourself.

The final stop on this crawl, Carmelina's, is a great destination before or after any North End snack.

10

ESCAPE TO SICILY AT CARMELINA'S

Sicily is one of my favorite places in Italy. The people are so warm, the island is so beautiful, and the food is so good. Sicilian food is made from the heart above all else.

The intimate dining space at **CARMELINA'S** reminds me of the busy trattorias in Italy. The feeling is intoxicating. The sounds of the kitchen and all the patrons laughing and enjoying themselves lift you up as soon as you step inside. And of course the food backs up this wonderful ambiance.

Carmelina's has just the right balance of hearty dishes and finessed plating. If you are a seafood lover, you need to try this place. I would hike all the way to the North End in a Nor'easter just for their Garlic Shrimp or the Tuna Arabiatta.

Oh and don't even get me started on the risotto—the creamy, cheesy goodness that it is. You need to try it for yourself.

This intimate restaurant has all the charm of the North End and all the flavors of southern Italy.

MANGIA!

The Theater District
Dinner and a Show

HAVING LIVED AROUND THE THEATER DISTRICT FOR SEVERAL YEARS, I have personally experienced the ups and downs that come from residing in an area to which people flock from all over the city for their nights out. Sometimes the street are packed, and sometimes I'm one of those people crowding the streets after the show gets out. But the crowds are just a part of daily life when you live in a city's theater district. I do love the fact that Boston has such a clearly defined Theater District. From the Wang to the Boston Opera House, the Theater District is filled to the brim with culture. The Theater District is the place to be when you're looking for dinner and a show. Now unrecognizable by its old nickname, the "Combat Zone," this is the coolest area of Boston. In an area that now has a W Hotel, a Ritz, and an Equinox, the Theater District is definitely a spot for the cool kids. With so many amazing hotspots, you just have to check it out!

THE THEATER DISTRICT CRAWL

1. **Be forever cool when you head to the W**
   100 STUART ST., BOSTON, (617) 261-8700, WBOSTON.COM/
   W-LOUNGE-BOSTON

2. **Sit above it all at BLU**
   4 AVERY ST., BOSTON, (617) 375-8550, BLURESTAURANT.COM

3. **Get ritzy at the RITZ CARLTON BOSTON**
   10 AVERY ST., BOSTON, (617) 574-7100, RITZCARLTON.COM/EN/HOTELS

4. **Grab dinner before the show at ARTISAN BISTRO**
   10 AVERY ST., BOSTON, (617) 574-7176, RITZCARLTON.COM/EN/HOTELS/
   BOSTON/DINING/ARTISAN-BISTRO

5. **Grab a tasty lunch at the downtown iteration of the old standby at
   LEGAL CROSSING**
   558 WASHINGTON ST., BOSTON, (617) 692-8888, LEGALSEAFOODS.COM/
   RESTAURANTS/BOSTON-LEGAL-CROSSING-25

6. **Tell them the redcoats are coming at the REVERE HOTEL**
   200 STUART ST., BOSTON, (617) 482-1800, REVEREHOTEL.COM/EAT-DRINK

7. **Party like it's a Tuesday at TUNNEL**
   100 STUART ST., BOSTON, (617) 357-5005, TUNNELBOSTON.COM

8. **Venture into the unknown at EXPLORATEUR**
   186 TREMONT ST., BOSTON, (617) 766-3179, EXPLORATEUR.COM

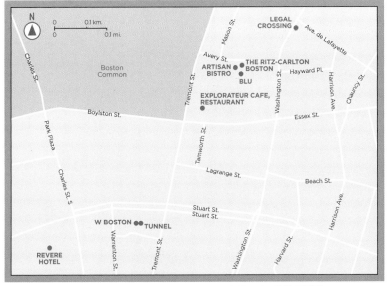

LET'S HEAD OUT TO DINNER AND A SHOW!

W HOTEL FACTS

- The W Hotel also has condos on the top half of the building, many with amazing views of the Common.

- One of the top spas in Boston, Bliss Spa, is located at the W.

- The hotel rooms are filled with chic décor.

- The Whatever/ Whenever service offered by the hotel is fantastic; you can ask for anything day or night!

1

BE FOREVER COOL WHEN YOU HEAD TO THE W

The **W** will always be my favorite spot in the Theater District, and it just keeps getting better. Let's start with the W Lounge. Instantly a hit since it opened a few years ago, the W Burger is always a good late night decision. And the seasonal cocktail menu could not be more fun. Still, my favorite drink remains the Lemongrass Drop.

There is a live DJ several nights a week, and the vibe is so cool you'll need a Canada Goose. W Lounge is the place you go when you want a guaranteed good time: good drinks, typical W Hotel décor (i.e. purple lighting and lots of metal), and a stylish crowd.

Next, let's get to the full-fledged restaurant, Gallery. Located in a space once occupied by a certain celebrity chef whom Boston wasn't quite ready for a few years ago, this place is now a funky small plates locale. So fun and so tasty, this menu is perfect for both happy hour apps or a full dinner on a Saturday night. Essentially, the W is the not-your-mother's-pre-theater-spot spot, as well as your after-work hangout, and the perfect place for your bachelorette party. Like I said, it's my favorite.

Another neighborhood favorite is Blu, which is a lovely restaurant with a view on the corner of Avery and Washington.

2 SIT ABOVE IT ALL AT BLU

On the same floor as the Equinox Sports Club at the Ritz Carton Boston, BLU is a hidden gem in every sense of the word. First, it has a sweeping view of Washington Street and the bustling life below. And second, it has a solid food and drink menu. Whether you are stopping in for a power lunch or a leisurely dinner with the significant other, Blu will leave you feeling like you stumbled upon a private supper club that only those in-the-know know about.

So now that you are in-the-know, what should you order? Well, the menu changes with the seasons, so ingredients are fresh and dishes are of-the-moment. You can always count on some interesting cocktails and the Roasted Chicken, which is a menu staple season after season. Pair your meal with that lovely view and you're ensured a perfect evening.

Next, head downstairs and up the street to the Avery Bar inside the Ritz for a classy night cap.

3

GET RITZY AT THE RITZ CARLTON BOSTON

The **RITZ CARLTON BOSTON** was one of the major changing forces in the Theater District. Cleaning up several blocks of the area all on its own, the hotel upped the amount of culture available to local residents. Its Avery Bar has been a happening place since it opened. And when you walk in you immediately realize you are in a Ritz Carlton. You get the sense that you simply need a glass of bubbly pronto.

Some bubbly or a bubbly-based cocktail paired with charcuterie is the play at Avery Bar. One of the coziest lobby bars around, you'll want to clear your calendar because once you sit down, it will be hard to leave! Well, except to head next door to the more laid back Artisan Bistro for dinner!

4

GRAB DINNER BEFORE THE SHOW AT ARTISAN BISTRO

The other dining location at the Ritz is the **ARTISAN BISTRO**, the more casual brother to the Avery Bar. The Artisan Bistro offers upscale American classics and a drink menu that packs a punch. Another fantastic pre- or post-theater option, the Artisan Bistro feels a world away from the bustling street outside. It's quiet, romantic, and relaxed. Whether you are partaking in a clandestine affair or a boys' night out, I highly recommend working the Artisan Bistro into your routine.

If you are going for a pre-theater bite, the menu at Artisan Bistro is quite tasty. The burrata and the scallops are fantastic, and you can also get the charcuterie board from Avery Bar served here as well.

If you are visiting the neighborhood, our next stop needs to be one of your lunchtime destinations.

5 GRAB A TASTY LUNCH AT THE DOWNTOWN ITERATION OF THE OLD STAND-BY AT LEGAL CROSSING

The Legal Seafood empire spans the country, and yet it continues to reinvent itself constantly. That has been the key to the success of the brand in its Boston home. Stemming from the flagship, Legal Harborside, **LEGAL CROSSING** was the funky answer to the new and improved Theater District.

Speaking to the heritage of the area, Legal Crossing is Legal with an Asian fusion twist. Don't worry, you can still get a lobster dinner here, but the menu is augmented with things like a play on a bipimbap and a hoisin-glazed salmon.

> "Legal Crossing and Legal Harborside are both inspired by their respective neighborhoods, Downtown Crossing and the Seaport District/Waterfront. While they offer very different experiences, both concepts share the same fanaticism for freshness and quality that will continue to drive our growth and evolution."
>
> — *Roger Berkowitz,*
> *Legal Sea Foods*
> *President & CEO*

The restaurant doesn't look or feel like any other Legal that you are used to. This certainly ain't your father's Legal Seafood. It's dark, mysterious, and has a funky menu. This is the Legal for the new generation. Oh and one thing people don't realize is that Legal Crossing has the perfect outdoor patio. So in the warmer months, when you're looking for an alfresco spot, head to Legal Crossing and snack on some seafood while you people watch!

Hop over to another cool spot in the Theater District, the Revere Hotel, which offers a few different options for drinking and eating.

TELL THEM THE REDCOATS ARE COMING AT THE REVERE HOTEL

Just down the street from the W, the **REVERE HOTEL** is something we never would have seen in Boston 10 years ago. It's a boutique hotel in a concrete building, with a rooftop pool and lounge and a funky lobby bar. Oh and it happens to be Paul Revere themed due to its proximity to Boston Common.

The Revere, which recently underwent a huge renovation in 2017, is quickly turning into one of my new favorite lobby bars in the city. With an enthusiastic and creative drinks program manager, the lobby bar is starting to make a name for itself. The drink menu is rotated out seasonally, and they are really taking advantage of the wonderful local sprits to which we have access around here. Those two things make for a dynamic menu that doesn't feel stale like so many hotel bars out there. Plus, the look and feel of the restaurant is just fab. I mean those cushions? Am I right?

And after you have warmed up at the Revere, head across the street to Tunnel for a night on the town!

7 PARTY LIKE IT'S A TUESDAY AT TUNNEL

The Theater District is not only home to the city's theaters but also its nightclubs. And while you might be thinking Boston doesn't really seem like the "clubbing" type of town, in this part of town it is! With all the students nearby, and many young professionals living close by as well, the nightlife scene on Stuart Street is popping.

But don't make fun of us, New Yorkers. Since Boston does have a limited number of nightclubs, each one has its special night of the week. For one of my favs, **TUNNEL**, Tuesday is its time in the sun. Tunnel Tuesdays do not disappoint. You'll have to check it out for yourself because you need to see it to believe it!

The subterranean nightclub is literally an underground tunnel with a twinkling ceiling that echoes the night sky. And it is one of the few clubs in town that employs a full-time light architect each night. Trust me, there is something about going out on a weeknight that keeps you young!

If you can't party on a Tuesday like you used to, next stop Explorateur has plenty of recovery fuel ready.

8 VENTURE INTO THE UNKNOWN AT EXPLORATEUR

The newest kid on the block, **EXPLORATEUR** ironically is in one of the oldest spots around. It's located in the Masonic building on the corner of Boylston and Tremont.

Taking cues from European cafés, Explorateur wants to be an all-day dining destination. You can come by in the morning for a coffee, stop in for a lunchtime salad, pop back in for a 3:00 p.m. snack, and then return at night for a full-dinner service.

It is an interesting spot. The architecture of the old building was enhanced and really brought to life. The restaurant is huge, yet it feels intimate because the different dining experiences are broken up very well. There's the café up front, with long study hall–style tables open for self-seating; the bar on the right; and the dining room on the back left-hand side.

Start with something fresh, either a salad or the crudo. Then go for the Explorateur Burger—it's big, it's juicy, and the fries are super crispy. Then finish with the crème brulee. Oh and be sure to come back for a cappuccino the next morning. The view from the café is great. Located right on the Common, you can get your fill of people watching anytime you want.

The Fenway and Allston

Fenway Frank Has Some Competition

FENWAY PARK IS A BOSTON TREASURE. Always a must for a first time (or 100th) visit to Boston, Fenway is an experience. Foodies have nothing to worry about in this neck of the woods, though— the Fenway Frank isn't your only culinary option. Fenway and Allston have some seriously funky hotspots. Everything from oysters to Asian fusion to tacos is available west of Massachusetts Avenue. Whether you're a Sophomore at BU or a hungry Sox fan, there is something for you. From old go-tos like Eastern Standard to fresh faces like Mei Mei, you won't be leaving hungry. But a word to my Bostonians: since I didn't have room in this book to cover Allston, Fenway, and the surrounding areas separately, please regard my neighborhood definition a little more loosely here than in the other chapters (I know I'm combining a few neighborhoods). From Island Creek to Tony C's, the western part of Boston isn't slacking when it comes to restaurants. When you explore Fenway and Allston the best part is that there are so many unexpected gems. Take a look at my top 7 picks!

THE FENWAY AND ALLSTON CRAWL

1. **Take your classy friend to EASTERN STANDARD**
   528 COMMONWEALTH AVE., BOSTON, (617) 532-9100,
   EASTERNSTANDARDBOSTON.COM

2. **Feast on everything raw at ISLAND CREEK OYSTER BAR**
   500 COMMONWEALTH AVE., BOSTON, (617) 532-5300,
   ISLANDCREEKOYSTERBAR.COM

3. **Live out your Fever Pitch dreams at TONY C'S**
   1265 BOYLSTON ST., BOSTON, (617) 236-7369, TONYCSSPORTSBAR.COM

4. **Live out your actual life at MEI MEI**
   506 PARK DR., BOSTON, (857) 250-4959, MEIMEIBOSTON.COM

5. **Get into it deep at DEEP ELLUM**
   477 CAMBRIDGE ST., ALLSTON, (617) 787-2337,
   DEEPELLUM-ALLSTON.COM/DEWP

6. **Head to HOJOKO, the funky after-game spot, for a change**
   1271 BOYLSTON ST., BOSTON, (617) 670-0507, HOJOKOBOSTON.COM

7. **Eat tacos with your BU friends at LONE STAR**
   479 CAMBRIDGE ST., BOSTON, (617) 782-8226,
   DEEPELLUM-ALLSTON.COM/LONESTAR

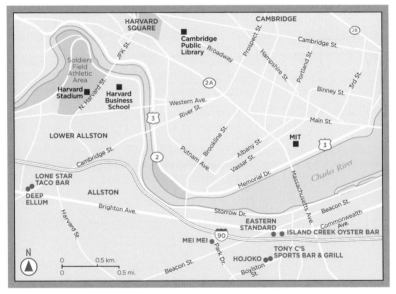

TAKE ME OUT TO THE BALLGAME!

1 TAKE YOUR CLASSY FRIEND TO EASTERN STANDARD

EASTERN STANDARD is the grand dame of everything west of Massachusetts Avenue. From alfresco cocktails to a post–Red Sox dinner, Eastern Standard is always a solid choice. They do well with the classics here. To all those other tartare lovers out there, ES makes a solid variation of this tasty classic.

The patio is one of the best and biggest in town. For all the Red Sox fans out there, Eastern Standard is right on the way to the ballpark.

So whether you are in the mood for a heartwarming bowl of baked pasta or a cocktail and some refreshing tartare, Eastern is the standard. And if you're feelin' fancy, I recommend the Roasted Bone Marrow!

Next door is the newer classic Island Creek Oyster Bar. Let's head to our next stop!

2 FEAST ON EVERYTHING RAW AT ISLAND CREEK OYSTER BAR

A newer icon in the area, **ISLAND CREEK OYSTER BAR** is the fresh-faced neighbor to Eastern Standard. Whereas Eastern Standard will warm your heart, Island Creek Oyster will chill you out. Responsible for turning Boston back on to oysters, Island Creek is the perfect place to acquire the taste for the little buggers if you haven't yet.

Not only does it offer a fresh product and well-executed menu, but Island Creek provides a high level of service and education in its approach to oysters. Something that once was unapproachable to the non-foodie is now so understandable, thanks in part to the nightly mini oyster education sessions that take place tableside

for so many diners. You should feel comfortable asking any server about the difference between the Wellfleet and Island Creek. They will explain everything in terms that we can all understand.

That being said, don't be afraid to dive right into the shellfish platter. It serves 4 and will please the whole table!

Like I said, Island Creek Oyster make oysters and their many different varieties accessible to the non-aficionado. These are a few of the popular varieties served up at the Island Creek raw bar.

But never fear, if there is someone who insists on ordering something cooked, go for the fabulously mouthwatering lobster roe noodles. They come with braised short rib, oyster mushrooms, and of course some lobster. Oh and starting off the night with some oyster sliders isn't a bad idea either.

While Island Creek is an excellent choice for pre- or post-Red Sox game, Tony C's is the quintessential spot for pre, post or during the game!

 LIVE OUT YOUR FEVER PITCH DREAMS AT TONY C'S

Sometimes the scene outside of Fenway Park is more exciting than the one inside. The bar scene surrounding the ballpark is phenomenal. With so many choices, each one rowdier than the next, the Fenway area is fun for both the baseball fan and the Boston pub fan.

TONY C'S on Boylston Street is rowdy before, during, and after games, so if you're looking for the traditional Boston sports bar scene, look no further. This is your spot. But unlike so many other

sports bars in the area, the food here is quite tasty. Combine that with the game on the flat screens and you could easily find yourself spending more time here than you originally planned.

Bring your appetite! Tony C's does a solid burger and, surprisingly, kale salad (which is absolutely ginormous, I might add!). And I highly recommend washing all that down with one of the margaritas. They are tangy and bright—just the way I like them!

If you aren't in the neighborhood for a game, perhaps just visiting BU or Northeastern, our next stop, Mei Mei is the place for you.

4

LIVE OUT YOUR ACTUAL LIFE AT MEI MEI

Boston has such a vibrant and diverse student population, and the Fenway/Allston neighborhoods are home to many of these students. As such there are so many satisfying restaurants in the area. But don't worry, these places aren't just suitable for the college kid up late working on his chem project. Boston's students must be foodies because they eat well in this part of town.

In addition to being one of the most recognizable food trucks, MEI MEI's brick and mortar location is also worth the hike. Serving up some tasty treats, Mei Mei's lamb dumplings and Jajang Noodle are the perfect dinner for anyone in need of something quick and delicious! Whether you want to sit and enjoy your meal at the restaurant or just grab and go, Mei Mei will delight any palate.

 **GET INTO IT DEEP AT DEEP ELLUM**

Allston may still be a college town, but at least the kids are eating better food these days. And at **DEEP ELLUM** they are also drinking better cocktails these days, too. Seriously, the proliferation of cocktail bars in Boston has exploded over the past few years. That combined with the craft beer scene makes Boston a certified booze hub in addition to a foodie hub. Our bartenders have literally raised the bar on themselves time and time again. And at Deep Ellum, when you see a petite lavender drink show up in a rough-and-tumble neighborhood like Allston, you know things are changing. Pair your cocktail with some solid bar food and you'll definitely make it through finals week with a smile!

I mean how can you begrudge anything after eating a giant warm Bavarian-style pretzel, served with cheese and mustard dip that anyone from Munich would approve of?

And if you happen to be a college kid in the area, heading to Fenway, our next stop is an alternative to all the typical pre- and post-game spots.

6 HEAD TO HOJOKO, THE FUNKY AFTER-GAME SPOT, FOR A CHANGE

The restaurant serving the Verb Hotel, HOJOKO is a whole new kind of funky. Taking cues from our nation's musical heritage, the hotel has a vibe that's unique to Boston. And Hojoko sees the funky and raises it to an Asian fusion level of cool. With plenty of sushi and sashimi on the menu, as well as some hearty poke bowl–style dishes, Hojoko is the place the cool kids go after a Sox game or on a regular old Tuesday night. It's just that cool.

Whether you want to grab a funky cocktail at the beautifully retro green bar or a burger in a booth, Hojoko is the spot for you in Fenway.

The Verb Hotel does retro cool in the best way. The view of the courtyard pool adds some flair to the dining room.

The Asian fusion fare is super tasty after a Sox game and really hits the spot on a cold night in the middle of January. To all the college kids who live in the area: This is a really cool spot to impress that foodie date!

But if you are dying for some tacos instead of Asian fusion, Lone Star is the spot for you.

7 EAT TACOS WITH YOUR BU FRIENDS AT LONE STAR

Who doesn't love a good taco? **LONE STAR** Taco is the answer to every college kid's late night dream.

The sister to Deep Ellum, Lone Star puts out some creative and downright delicious tacos, tostadas, and margaritas. Whether you are stopping in for a nice brunch or finishing off the night, Lone Star delivers on both the cool and the taste. Oh and the cooper bar adds a major dash of old world devil-may-care attitude that fits the neighborhood perfectly, and I like that.

Start off the meal with a bowl of guac and some chips. I love how the guac is served: in a giant mortar bowl. Then move on to a series of tacos. My recommendation is to go crazy. They are priced individually, so you are forced to break out of your comfort zone and pick a few different ones if you want a full meal. My approach in this situation is to cover all the bases: something with meat, something with seafood, and something with veggies. I mean the taco diet should be well balanced!

East Boston

Hola Amigo & Ciao Regazzi: Tacos and Pizza, What More Could You Need?

THE THEME OF THIS BOOK IS CHANGE. Boston is a changing city and has been for the past few years. After decades of staying the same, something happened a few years ago and all of a sudden the city started to grow. Now a bastion of young professionals, all of Boston's neighborhoods have undergone some degree of gentrification. And the one that is most drastically on that path right now is East Boston, or "Eastie" as we like to call it around here. Eastie is a juxtaposition of new condo buildings and family-owned establishments. And all that means good things for the food scene in the neighborhood. Family-owned eateries are thriving right alongside the newer hot spots cropping up. If you haven't ventured onto the Blue Line just yet, now is the time to make the jump! With views of the Boston skyline and some amazing restaurants, Eastie is the new hot neighborhood. Hop on the train and check out these amazing places, I mean come on: you can get authentic Latin American cuisine, thin crust pizza, or a waterfront cocktail!

THE EAST BOSTON CRAWL

1. **New Eastie: REELHOUSE**
   6 NEW ST., BOSTON, (617) 895-4075, REELHOUSEBOSTON.COM

2. **Old Eastie: SANTARPIO'S PIZZA**
   111 CHELSEA ST., BOSTON, (617) 567-9871, SANTARPIOSPIZZA.COM

3. **South of the border Eastie: TAQUERIA JALISCO**
   291 BENNINGTON ST., BOSTON, (617) 567-6367

4. **Head to the land down under at KO CATERING AND PIES**
   256 MARGINAL ST., #16, BOSTON, (617) 418-5234, KOCATERINGANDPIES.COM

5. **Head to Peru via RINCON LIMEÑO**
   409 CHELSEA ST., EAST BOSTON, (617) 569-4942, RINCONLIMENO.COM

6. **Eat all you can at OLIVEIRA'S**
   297 CHELSEA ST., EAST BOSTON, (617) 561-7277,
   OLIVEIRASRESTAURANT.COM

7. **Make Mondays for margaritas again at ANGELA'S CAFÉ**
   131 LEXINGTON ST., BOSTON, (617) 567-4972, ANGELASCAFEBOSTON.COM

8. **Hang with the cool kids at CUNARD TAVERN**
   24 ORLEANS ST., BOSTON, (617) 567-7609, CUNARDTAVERN.COM

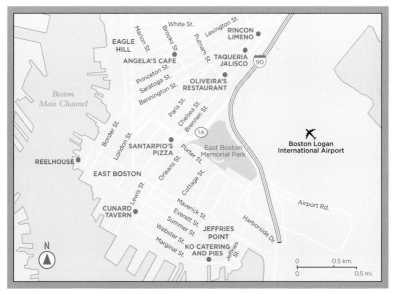

LET'S HEAD TO EASTIE!

1

NEW EASTIE: REELHOUSE

Following in the footsteps of Southie, Eastie has attracted many recent college grads and young families. A convenient yet relatively affordable option close to downtown Boston, Eastie is currently undergoing a surge in popularity for newcomers to Boston, and the construction rate of new condos and apartment buildings is doing its best to keep up. One of the recent by-products of all these new dollars coming to the neighborhood is **REELHOUSE**. Located on the street level of one of the new condo buildings, Reelhouse is an upscale waterfront restaurant that is just a dream come sunset. The views of the Boston skyline are unreal, and the sea breeze is the most pleasant thing you will experience all day. That combined with a delicious tiki drink makes for the perfect way to unwind after work.

The view is seriously a stunner, and the food isn't bad either. Rightly focusing on seafood, Reelhouse is a fun place for drinks on a warm summer afternoon or even on a cool October night. With both an outdoor terrace and an outdoor bar, Reelhouse was built for alfresco fun.

And come the cooler months, the actual restaurant itself was built to take in the amazing views. With floor-to-ceiling windows all around, you can ogle Boston all you want throughout dinner.

Next up, we have Santarpio's, which is Eastie's answer to Pizzeria Regina.

2

OLD EASTIE: SANTARPIO'S PIZZA

The battle continues to wage on. Who does it better, **SANTARPIO'S** or Regina? Depending on who you ask you'll get a different answer. There are pros and cons to each. At Santarpio's you're getting something you can't get anywhere else. It's the closest thing to New York-style pizza you're going to

get in Boston. If you want to experience "old Eastie," you have to stop by this pizza joint. The line can be long, so be prepared to wait for your pie.

For longtime East Boston residents, Santarpio's is an institution. And for Boston foodies, it has become one location in the great pizza debate pilgrimage. The only way to make up your mind for yourself is to jump on the Blue Line to go check it out!

But a few pro tips. First, know which entrance you are looking for. There is a takeout door and a restaurant door. Next, there is only one size for all the pizzas, so don't be asking for a medium. And finally, bring cash because the last time I checked it was still cash only.

But all of this is worth it, even the Blue Line hike, because the pizza crust is thin and crispy—just as it should be!

Another spot worth the hike is Taqueria Jalisco. Read on to find out why!

3 SOUTH OF THE BORDER EASTIE: TAQUERIA JALISCO

Eastie is proudly the home of a large Latin and Central American immigrant population and therefore is the spot to grab some amazing authentic Central and Latin American cuisine. One of my favorites is **TAQUERIA JALISCO** on Bennington Street.

A colorful mom and pop place, you can get all the classics here: tacos, sopes, and burritos. But the real gem is the trio of hot sauces that accompanies your meal. When the server brings those out, you know you are somewhere legit. Seriously you have to try them all. With a staff so friendly and inviting, you'll never go anywhere else for tacos again.

What to order? Go for the trio of tacos with rice and beans, a sope, and some Tres Leches for dessert. The classics are on point. And like I said, once you try the hot sauces on the tacos, this will become your new go-to taco spot.

Oh and an added bonus is that they deliver!

Eastie is filled with delicious authentic ethnic cuisines, and one that may not be on people's radar is Aussie street food. KO Pies is doing some amazing things with their handheld pies; they are next on our list!

4 HEAD TO THE LAND DOWN UNDER AT KO CATERING AND PIES

Eastie is such an interesting place. On one hand you have the classics like Santarpio's, and on the other you have new spots like **KO CATERING AND PIES**. Run by some Aussies, KO Pies serves up traditional Aussie hand pies and beer, and you can consume these on the lovely outdoor covered deck just as nature intended. If you've never had a traditional Australian "hand pie," it is exactly what it sounds like: a pint-sized pie. And they even have a sign on the premises telling you how to eat it. I mean seriously, it's a pie, mate!

All the pies are savory, and honestly you can't go wrong on the flavors! We tried the classic beef, Irish beef stew, and the pie of the month (lamb). Just go for it.

And if you're still wondering how to eat it, you can either pick it up and take a bite, cut it in half and take a bite, or use a fork and knife the whole time. But once you dig into these little things, you'll want to just pick them up. They're called "hand pies" after all.

KO Pies in Eastie is located right in the shipyard, which adds to the relevance of such a rustic thing as a pie. You're in a shipyard, so a dainty plate wouldn't make sense. But a pie that you can eat with your hands outside? It's perfect. Oh and you do get that nice sea view and breeze while you're sitting on the KO Pie patio.

The next stop Rincon Limeno, is a fabulous Peruvian haunt.

HEAD TO PERU VIA RINCON LIMEÑO

Like I mentioned, Eastie is home to a large Latin and Central American population. And **RINCON LIMEÑO** brings us the flavors of Peru. With everything from ceviche to pisco to tacu tacu, Rincon Limeno has all the classics.

The traditional food of Peru is full of flavor. And as big fans of seafood, the Peruvians brought ceviche to the world. As we all know ceviche is the amazing raw, marinated preparation of seafood that is so popular today.

Starting with a big dish of their amazing ceviche is the right way to begin a meal at Rincon Limeno. And from there you need to try one of the traditional entrees they are also serving up. The tacu tacu is a bean and seafood dish with an amazing cream sauce poured on top. With shrimp, squid, and mussels as the stars, this dish is a delightful seafood medley. To wash that down, a tasty pisco cocktail is required.

For more Latin flavor, head to Oliviera's, a Brazilian Steakhouse in the neighborhood.

6

EAT ALL YOU CAN AT OLIVEIRA'S

Who doesn't love a good all-you-can-eat steakhouse? And an all-you-can-eat Brazilian steakhouse is even better! As part of your Latin American food tour of Eastie, you just have to check out **OLIVEIRA'S**.

Located on Chelsea Street about halfway up Eastie, the restaurant has an unassuming façade but makes up for it in flavor. But beware: come hungry because you will not be leaving without a full belly.

One more spot to get your fill of tasty Latin flavors is Angela's Café, located on Eagle Hill.

7

MAKE MONDAYS FOR MARGARITAS AGAIN AT ANGELA'S CAFÉ

Finally, my last recommendation for Eastie is **ANGELA'S CAFE**, which has two locations in the area, one on Eagle Hill and another in Orient Heights.

Angela's is a classic Mexican cantina–style restaurant. Serving up traditional Mexican food from the city of Puebla, things like pipián and chilaquiles are must-trys. And no matter what you get, you have to try the margaritas. There are several different options: Traditional (with a kick), strawberry, or coconut. I have to say that I would make the trip back to Eastie just for the chilaquiles with a coconut margarita; the creamy margarita was the perfect foil to the tasty chilaquiles.

So let's all pitch in and make margarita Mondays a thing again by heading to **ANGELA'S** for some traditional Puebla cuisine!

And after you get your fill of delicious Latin flavors, head over to our last stop in Eastie, the newest kid on the block, Cunard Tavern.

HANG WITH THE COOL KIDS AT CUNARD TAVERN

While Southie has that frat bro vibe, Eastie is more hipster cool. And **CUNARD TAVERN** is the restaurant incarnation of that very vibe. Both eclectic and direct, Cunard is the spot that you will keep going back to again and again. The food, the drinks, and the atmosphere are defining forces in the neighborhood right now. And for some recent grads, this place could honestly be enough to con-

vince them it's worth the move over the harbor.

Picture-perfect cocktails paired with a relaxed menu are exactly what we want from restaurants these days, and Cunard has this down to a tee.

The whole menu is filled with refined new American comfort food; things like Waffle Sliders and Grilled Scallops with Lobster Salad just make so much sense for Eastie. And there is even a dessert centered on the New England favorite: fluff! The Fluff and Peanut Butter Beignet is an upscale throwback to all those childhood flavors. And it is definitely worth a try!

If Cunard is any harbinger of what is to come for the neighborhood, Eastie could quickly turn into Boston's Brooklyn! So head over to Eastie to see what all the buzz is about. Cunard Tavern is waiting to be your next favorite neighborhood spot.

The Cambridge Crawl
Funky Fancy Fusion

WHILE THERE WASN'T ROOM TO DO CAMBRIDGE JUSTICE IN THIS BOOK, there was no way I wasn't going to at least give it a nod. Cambridge is like Boston's cool older brother. Cambridge always has all the cool stuff before the rest of us. From Asian fusion, to fancy tasting menus to funky cocktails, Cambridge does it all. I discover something new every time I venture over the Charles. From the molecular magic at Café Art Science to the fancy fusion at Pagu, Cambridge is a foodie's dream. Each of Cambridge's neighborhoods has its own personality, just like Boston's. They each deserve a special trip, but this crawl will introduce you to some of the best highlights. From Central to Harvard to Porter, each square has something different to offer. I only get to touch on the major neighborhoods here, so you'll just have to go check them out for yourself. Here are a few highlights from this amazing foodie city just over the Charles.

THE CAMBRIDGE CRAWL

1. **Study up on craft cocktails at** CAFÉ ART SCIENCE
   650 E. KENDALL ST., CAMBRIDGE, (857) 999-2193, CAFEARTSCIENCE.COM

2. **Get a degree in Asian fusion at** PAGU
   310 MASSACHUSETTS AVE., CAMBRIDGE, (617) 945-9290, GOPAGU.COM

3. **Work toward your masters in sushi at** THELONIOUS MONKFISH
   524 MASSACHUSETTS AVE., CAMBRIDGE, (617) 441-2116,
   THELONIOUSMONKFISH.COM

4. **Break out your flask at the** LITTLE DONKEY
   505 MASSACHUSETTS AVE., CAMBRIDGE, (617) 945-1008,
   LITTLEDONKEYBOS.COM

5. **Settle down for a romantic dinner at** CRAIGIE ON MAIN
   853 MAIN ST., CAMBRIDGE, (617) 497-5511, CRAIGIEONMAIN.COM

6. **Pull an all-nighter with a little help from** AREA FOUR
   500 TECHNOLOGY SQUARE, CAMBRIDGE, (617) 758-4444, AREAFOUR.COM

7. **Reward yourself with a beer at** KIRKLAND TAP AND TROTTER
   425 WASHINGTON ST., SOMERVILLE, (857) 259-6585,
   KIRKLANDTAPANDTROTTER.COM

8. **Celebrate with your friends at** ALDEN AND HARLOW
   40 BRATTLE ST., CAMBRIDGE, (617) 864-2100, ALDENHARLOW.COM

9. **Bring your parents to** LES SABLONS
   2 BENNETT ST., CAMBRIDGE, (617) 268-6800, LSCAMBRIDGE.COM

10. **Mix it up at** BEAT BRASSERIE
    13 BRATTLE ST., CAMBRIDGE, (617) 499-0001, BEATBRASSERIE.COM

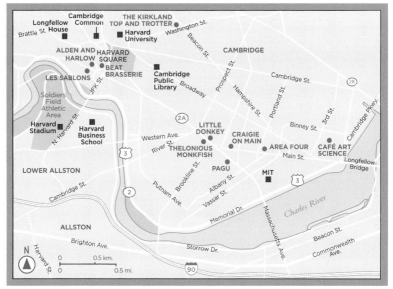

LET'S HEAD TO CAMBRIDGE!

1

STUDY UP ON CRAFT COCKTAILS AT CAFÉ ART SCIENCE

Cambridge has such an amazing food scene and has generally been a little more avant garde than Boston. **CAFÉ ART SCIENCE** keeps up with that tradition. Located in the heart of Kendall Square, Café Art Science really plays to the fact that it is literally on the MIT campus. It boasts intelligent menus; when I last visited, the drinks were named after endangered animals, and the events calendar was set up like a course syllabus. Details like that are all part of the charm.

But what about this whole "art" and "science" thing? Well as for the art, the restaurant has invested in some very forward-thinking pieces by local artists. And oftentimes those pieces involve quite a bit of science; for example, a dramatic representation of a pill that was recently on display.

As the brainchild of Dr. David Edwards, a Harvard professor, Café Art Science is a place for innovation when it comes to culture, food, and drinks. But don't let all these buzzwords fool you; they are serious when it comes to flavor, not just appearances.

The drinks on the menu are probably the most exciting you will find anywhere in Massachusetts.

And while I'd say that the drinks are the star of the show, the food is certainly a powerful supporting actor. Both artistic and scientific, Café Art Science will increase the IQ of both the left and right sides of your brain!

After your science lesson, head to Chef Tracy's flavor academy at Pagu.

2 GET A DEGREE IN ASIAN FU-SION AT PAGU

An alum of O Ya and co-creator of Guchi's Midnight Ramen, Chef Tracy Chang was not messing around when she opened **PAGU** on Mass. Ave. in 2016.

If you have one meal to eat in Cambridge, it must be at Pagu. The perfect fusion of Japanese and Spanish cuisines, Pagu packs a powerful punch to the taste buds. With each dish more full of flavor than the last, the seasonal menu does not disappoint.

A few mainstays have lasted through the first few seasons the restaurant has been open. The Squid Ink Bao Bao and the Ramen are absolute must-trys. But the real way to dine here is the prix fixe menu. The set menu delivers everything you hoped it would. Often starting with something raw, then moving to a hot pintxos, then on to some bao, then to a main course, and finally to dessert, you are brought on a harmonious

"Central Square is a lovely melting pot of people and cultures. Having lived and worked in Spain, tapas is close to my heart. That, combined with growing up in my grandmother's Japanese restaurant, a celebration of cultures was what I wanted Pagu to be."

– *Tracy Chang, chef & owner*

international culinary journey that leaves you utterly delighted.

In between Kendall and Central Squares, the location certainly attracts a lot of cool kids. And with several cool kid-approved seating areas—the bar, the chef's counter, the patio, and the main dining room—Pagu offers many experiences you can choose from based on what you're feeling that night. Do you want to catch up with an old friend at the bar over a crafty creation? Or do you want to have a fun date night at the chef's counter? Or maybe it is a beautiful evening and you want to take it all in from the patio. No matter what, you are going to leave wanting to come back again and again!

Next up is Thelonious Monkfish, the spot for sushi in Central Square.

WORKS TOWARD YOUR MASTERS IN SUSHI AT THELONIOUS MONKFISH

Masters of the intricate sushi roll, **THELONIOUS MONKFISH** is the place to go when you just need more maki in your life.

They make sushi dreams here—literally. With a whole section of the menu called Fairytale Sushi, it's not hard to see why. From Snow White to Sleeping Beauty, you can feel like your favorite Disney princess while gorging on sushi. It doesn't get much better than that. And the sushi even matches the vibe of each princess; you get a crisp Snow White and a gorgeous Sleeping Beauty.

And with live jazz performances several times a week, Thelonious Monkfish is a great casual spot to hang out if you're looking for some yummy sushi and a relaxed atmosphere.

The curries, noodles, and rice dishes are also well worth the trip over the bridge!

4

BREAK OUT YOUR FLASK AT THE LITTLE DONKEY

Another notch in the belts of Ken Oringer and Jamie Bissonnette, **LITTLE DONKEY** in Central Square is one of those places that is always going to be hard to get a table at, no matter what time you show up. And that's what you call buzz. This is the place to be in Central Square. With crazy drinks like the daily Flask Special or the One that Comes in a Grapefruit, the fun starts as soon as you sit down.

With a funky small plates menu, you really can't go wrong. Be brave and pick one from each section of the menu, then ooh and ah when it arrives. Even things that sound simple, like Cucumber Salad, come with a twist at the Little Donkey.

Oh and don't skip the raw bar. With several ceviches, tartars, and pokes to choose from, you'll definitely want to start off your meal with something fresh.

And once you've opened up your palate, heavier-duty items like blowfish and the Istanbul-Style Manti Dumplings are what you'll be craving. The Little Donkey isn't so little when it comes to flavor; in fact, it donkey kicks you right in the face! The inevitable wait will be worth it, I promise.

Cambridge has so many worthy restaurants, you can't stop yet! Next up on our list is Craigie on Main.

"Travel is the key inspiration to this menu. Both Ken and I have been lucky enough to visit some pretty amazing cities and countries, and most items on the Little Donkey menu have been inspired by one of these trips. We'll fall in love with a dish abroad and then find a way to incorporate a piece of that with our own technique here."

– Jamie Bissonnette, chef/partner

5

SETTLE DOWN FOR A ROMANTIC DINNER AT CRAIGIE ON MAIN

Chef Tony Maws' **CRAIGIE ON MAIN** is a sophisticated Cambridge mainstay. Close to MIT and Central Square, this is where you need to go for a romantic night out with your special someone.

The way to go here is the prix fixe menu. Taking you through the highlights of everything they have to offer, the set menu will ensure that you get to try a little of everything. And don't forget the cocktails. The bar program is just as amazing as the food. The strong, purposeful drinks leave just as much of a mark on you as the food and will leave you wanting more.

My favorite part about Craigie on Main is that the set menu satisfies but doesn't overindulge. I've had so many tasting menus and chef's menus that leave you stuffed to the brink, but this one leaves you wanting one more bite. Which is exactly how it should.

The quality of ingredients is apparent in each and every bite. I think it's safe to say that it is indeed #lit.

On Sunday nights after 9:00 p.m., the only menu offered is the Chef's Whim, and the only rule is that it's different every week. They

"We look at ingredients first, then come up with concepts for dishes. And the Chef's Whim is a chance for us to push the envelope."

–Tony Maws, chef

craft the menu from ingredients that aren't used in the regular dinner service that night. The menu promises some funky creations weekly.

Next up, is something a little more casual, Area Four, which offers some of the best crispy thin crust pizza in town.

6

PULL AN ALL-NIGHTER WITH A LITTLE HELP FROM AREA FOUR

It shouldn't surprise you that an area with probably more students per square foot than anywhere else in the state has a fantastic pizza joint. But **AREA FOUR** is so much more than your local pizza parlor. They serve crispy, creative, thin crust pizzas that remind me of the ones you get in Naples—that slight char balancing well with the creamy, cheesy toppings.

So if you need a pick-me-up during a big study sesh or want to celebrate finishing a final, Area Four has got you covered. You can count on plenty of tasty options to slate your hunger.

Also, their cocktails aren't bad either. You could definitely make a night of it at Area Four, and better yet, if you're not up for that, they also do takeout!

7 REWARD YOURSELF WITH A BEER AT KIRKLAND TAP AND TROTTER

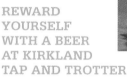

Craigie on Main's chill brother, **KIRKLAND TAP AND TROTTER** near Inman Square, is a cool neighborhood-y spot. It's definitely somewhere that you could post up on a Sunday afternoon but also a place to start your Friday night. Kirkland Tap and Trotter has got it all figured out.

The biggest draw is the roast chicken. "Winner, winner, chicken dinner," you can get their chicken dinners to go or to stay. You thought you knew chicken before, but trust me, you've never had chicken like this. A piece of perfectly cooked chicken is a rare commodity. Too often chicken is dry and overcooked, but Tony's is perfect. His team must have it down to a science.

This chicken comes roasted just so, with some quinoa and cilantro-heavy salsa verde. It is absolutely delectable. And for all my Bostonians who are worried Cambridge and Somerville are "so far," trust me when I say that after you've tried this chicken, you will never think twice about making the trek again.

While the chicken is most certainly the star, everything on the menu is delicious. The burger hits the spot and so do the mussels.

For more elevated classics, Alden and Harlow in Harvard Square is a must! Read on to see why.

 **CELEBRATE WITH YOUR FRIENDS AT
ALDEN AND HARLOW**

I have to admit it, I have a soft spot for Harvard Square. Something about it is just so special—the historic buildings, the energy, and the culture. And with all of that comes some amazing restaurants. One of the crowd favorites is **ALDEN AND HARLOW**. The place to celebrate anything with a group of friends, the food and drinks will keep you lingering for hours.

By now we have all heard about the Secret Burger, so I'm not so sure how secret it is anymore. Regardless it is a must-try. The sauce and accoutrements make for one of the best burgers in town. Pair that with either the pancakes or the burrata as an app and you've got yourself a meal!

But there are so many other items of note on the menu; even something as simple as the charred broccoli is out of this world. The butternut puree with crushed nuts on top take it up a notch. So I guess it really is possible to get your veggies while keeping your taste buds happy.

How are the drinks? I could go on all day about the drinks. With a cocktail menu that is refreshed often, the offerings are always seasonal. That combined with top-shelf ingredients and creative bartenders—you are in for a treat, even if you just pop in for a drink.

The penultimate spot on this list, goes to Les Sablons, which is another Harvard Square favorite.

9 BRING YOUR PARENTS TO LES SABLONS

Looking for somewhere fancy to take your parents when they're in town? **LES SABLONS** is just the place. Also right in Harvard Square, the restaurant is an upscale eatery that takes each dish so seriously you'd think someone's life depended on it.

Meticulous doesn't even do it justice. I mean just check out that Rye Spaghetti pictured above.

But seriously, this is a cool place too. The marble bar is amazing, and the cocktails are to match. Oh and did I mention that this was in Harvard Square? Just the zip code gives it an extra dose of chic. A place like this could easily feel overdone, yet when dining here you still feel just as relaxed as if you were at your neighborhood bistro.

Finally, if you are looking to change up your routine, Harvard Square has the answer again with Beat Brasserie.

10

Those people who say Cambridge is a little too upscale these days or a little too coddled and that its old funky self is long gone haven't been to **BEAT BRASSERIE**. Just as its name suggests, this restaurant puts a big focus on music. With live music most of the week, Beat Brasserie feels more like a tiki-themed speakeasy in Brooklyn rather than a restaurant in Cambridge. And we like it that way!

The drinks are fun, the service is attentive, and the food is tasty. What more could you want? Head here if you are looking for a way out of your Saturday night rut. Mix it up at Beat Brasserie and you won't be disappointed.

Bonus Crawl!

The Classic Chowder

CHOWDER IS ABOUT AS BOSTON AS IT GETS. And while we are a hip, trendy city these days, with glamorous high-rises and food trucks, we still like our chowder. Theses classics are musts for anyone new to the Boston food scene.

THE CHOWDER CRAWL

NO NAME

15½ FISH PIER ST. E., BOSTON, (617) 423-2705, NONAMERESTAURANT.COM

UNION OYSTER HOUSE

41 UNION ST., BOSTON, (617) 227-2750, UNIONOYSTERHOUSE.COM

PARKER'S RESTAURANT

60 SCHOOL ST., BOSTON, (617) 725-1600, OMNIHOTELS.COM/HOTELS/BOSTON-PARKER-HOUSE/DINING/PARKERS-RESTAURANT

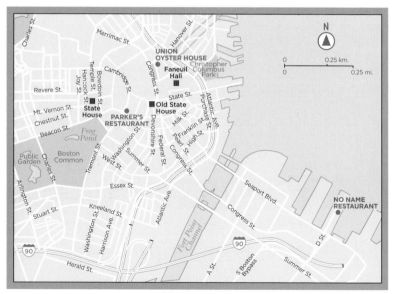

LET'S GET OUR CHOWDER ON!

1 THE NO NAME

If you just came to Boston for the chowder, then the **NO NAME** has to be your first stop.

As you learned in the Seaport Crawl, once a lunch counter for hungry dock workers, the No Name is the longest continually operating family-run business in Boston. Founder Nick Contos refused to name the restaurant, so it eventually became known as the restaurant with no name and then, affectionately, the No Name.

The No Name serves up classic seafood dishes, but the one you have to try is the fish chowder. It's not clam chowder; rather, it has several different seafoods involved. And on a cold day in Boston, it definitely hits the spot!

2 UNION OYSTER HOUSE

The next classic Boston restaurant that you must head to when you're craving some chowder is **UNION OYSTER HOUSE**. Here you can get some of the classic clam chowder New England is so famous for.

The oldest restaurant in America, Union Oyster House has hosted its fair share of celebrities and presidents. In fact, you can even sit in President John F. Kennedy's favorite old booth.

But the main attraction here is the clam chowder. Creamy and rich, it is everything you would expect in a New England–style chowder. That combined with the history of the place makes this a must-see on any Boston food crawl.

And finally, the 3rd spot for a classic chowder is Parker's Restaurant inside the Omni Parker House Hotel.

3

PARKER'S RESTAURANT

Located in the Omni Parker House Hotel, **PARKER'S RESTAURANT** is another old pillar of the Boston food scene. Once the place where the movers and shakers in town would power lunch, Parker's has some great stories tied to it. Not only is it the birthplace of the Parker House Roll and Boston Crème Pie, but it also does a mean clam chowder!

So if you aren't too full from your cups at the No Name and Union Oyster House, head to Parker's for number 3. And this being Boston, of course there is another JFK reference here: table 40 is where he proposed to Jacqueline Bouvier.

But the cool stories don't stop there. Both Ho Chi Minh and Malcolm X worked at the hotel at some point in their lives. Oh and by the way, it's haunted. Yes, haunted. Sightings of a man in 1800s dress have been reported throughout the hotel, as have several other spooky happenings. But you'll have to go there and check it out for yourself.

Bonus Crawl!

Best Rooftops

Boston has not traditionally been known as the fun drinks-on-the-roof type of place. But that's all changing. There are many beautiful places that offer amazing rooftops, some in the summer only and some year round!

THE ROOFTOP CRAWL

LOOKOUT ROOFTOP BAR
70 SLEEPER ST., BOSTON, (617) 338-3030, OUTLOOKKITCHENANDBAR.COM

YOTEL
65 SEAPORT BLVD., BOSTON, (617) 377-4747, YOTEL.COM/EN/HOTELS/YOTEL-BOSTON/EAT-AND-DRINK

ROOFTOP@REVERE
200 STUART ST., BOSTON, (855) 673-8373, REVEREHOTEL.COM/EAT-DRINK/ROOFTOP-REVERE

THE COLONNADE HOTEL
120 HUNTINGTON AVE., BOSTON, (617) 424-7000, COLONNADEHOTEL.COM

EQUINOX SPORTS CLUB BOSTON
4 AVERY ST., BOSTON, (617) 375-8200, EQUINOX.COM/CLUBS/BOSTON/SPORTSCLUBBOSTON

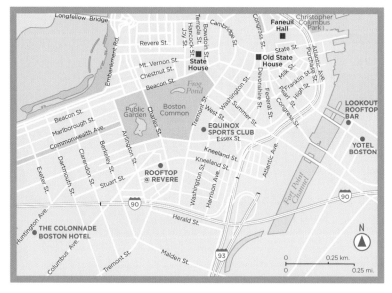

LET'S GO ROOFTOP HOPPING!

LOOKOUT ROOFTOP BAR

The rooftop at the Envoy Hotel, the **LOOKOUT ROOFTOP BAR** is the place to be in the summer. It is one of the defining locales of the Seaport.

But as I mentioned in my Seaport chapter, the real play here is to have dinner at Outlook on the ground floor of the restaurant and then head up to the roof for drinks.

But anytime you head to Envoy on a nice night, expect a line. This is a hot spot, so you may have to wait a little bit to get in. I promise it's worth it—the views, the crowd, and the scene are all top notch!

Next up, is a new spot just a hop skip and a jump from the Envoy—Yotel.

2

SKY LOUNGE
AT YOTEL

The new kid on the block, **YOTEL** is another Seaport rooftop option. Another great spot for a beautiful summer evening outside, Yotel also offers nice views of the Boston skyline and the Seaport. But one major fun fact about this venue is that it is a year-round destination. With indoor and outdoor seating, Yotel caters to Bostonians looking for drinks with a view no matter the season. So if it's the middle of January and you need to get out of the house, go grab a hot toddy and enjoy the view from Yotel Sky Lounge. But if you are lucky enough to be in Boston in the summertime, I think a visit to a rooftop pool is in order and both the Revere and Colonnade Hotels have ones that are open to the public.

3

ROOFTOP@ REVERE

ROOFTOP@REVERE is the Theater District's answer to Envoy. This is the spot in the summer for late night parties or daytime pool bashes (yes there is a rooftop pool!).

So grab a bunch of friends, reserve a cabana, get a bottle of bubbly, and pretend you're in the South of France. Revere has the party vibe nailed. The DJs and drinks are always on point. But with a hot spot comes hot spot lines, so come early if you don't want to wait.

4 THE COLONNADE HOTEL

The **COLONNADE HOTEL** has the most beautiful outdoor rooftop pool (the Revere's is on the roof but is indoors). There is something so special about a pool on the roof. You just feel on top of the world. How fabulous is that?

Serving up tasty food and drinks (with many frozen options), the Colonnade is a great place to hang with friends on a sunny summer day and linger into the night!

And finally, the next rooftop doesn't have a pool but it does have a great view!

EQUINOX SPORTS CLUB BOSTON

This last rooftop is a bit of an insider's secret and is not technically open to the public. But I thought I would throw in something for all my Bostonians reading this. We all know Equinox is the premier fitness club in the city, and with so many beautiful locations, it can be hard to choose which one to join. Here is my case for the **EQUINOX SPORTS CLUB BOSTON** location in the Theater District on Avery Street: its roof deck. After a hard workout, there is something magical about coming up here to relax and enjoy the view. While this may not have the same appeal as Envoy or Yotel (ahem, no drinks served, except when they host events), I can't think of a better place in Boston to enjoy a cold glass of water! Check it out. It certainly makes getting yourself to the gym a little bit easier.

Bonus Crawl!
Late-Afternoon Lattes

LIKE I MENTIONED IN THE CHAPTERS ON DOWNTOWN AND THE THEATER DISTRICT, this area of Boston is one that has changed the most drastically from what it once was. Once dangerous, Downtown is now a chic, desirable place to live. And as I'm about to demonstrate, it's filled with stylish, high-end coffee shops and bakeries.

THE LATTE CRAWL

JAHO COFFEE ROASTER AND WINE BAR
665 WASHINGTON ST., BOSTON, (857) 233-4094, JAHO.COM

BAO BAO BAKERY
84 HARRISON AVE., BOSTON, 617-988-8191

OGAWA COFFEE
10 MILK ST., BOSTON, (617) 780-7139, OGAWACOFFEEUSA.COM

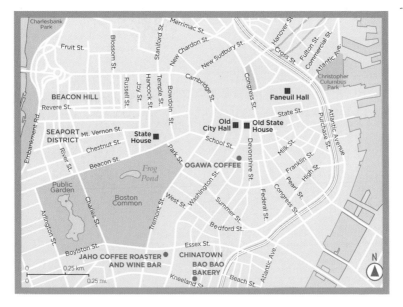

THESE 3 ARE MY TOP PICKS FOR BOSTON COFFEE SHOPS. LET'S CHECK THEM OUT!

1 JAHO COFFEE ROASTER AND WINE BAR

We'll start this latte crawl in Chinatown with **JAHO COFFEE ROASTER AND WINE BAR**. Housed in the Kensington apartment building, Jaho is a coffeehouse by day and wine bar by night.

Serving up some tasty lattes and cappuccinos, Jaho is the spot to grab a coffee after a delicious dinner at one of the many amazing restaurants in Chinatown. And it even has a little outdoor seating for use during the summer months. Or take your coffee to go to enjoy with a sweet treat at Chinatown neighbor Bao Bao.

2 BAO BAO BAKERY

While you're in Chinatown, **BAO BAO BAKERY** is a fantastic little hidden gem. Serving up so many colorful, tasty treats, the bakery is the place to go when you are looking for something out of the ordinary. Whether you need a gift for a foodie hostess or a colorful cake for a child's birthday party, Bao Bao will surprise and delight.

Besides their wonderful pastry case, Bao Bao Bakery also has a full wall of delectable Asian-style breads and buns, as well as a full-service drinks counter. With everything from bubble tea to smoothies, if you are craving something sweet and delicious this afternoon, Bao Bao will certainly wet your whistle. When the sugar and caffeine buzz starts to wear off, next stop Ogawa has got you covered.

3 OGAWA COFFEE

OGAWA COFFEE comes to us all the way from Japan. And with it comes some of that famous Japanese cool factor. From the interesting stadium seating to the elaborate drinks, Ogawa is a spot for the cool kids.

Its most Instagramable offering is the seasonal latte art. With things from jack-o-lanterns to animals, these coffee slingers are not messing around. The talented baristas and quality coffee will keep you coming back again and again.

Appendix: Eateries by Cuisine & Specialty

Asian
Artisan Bistro, 130
Banyan Bar +
  Refuge, 60
BLR, 102
Bubor Cha Cha, 100
China Pearl, 107
Crave-Mad For
  Chicken, 106
Double Chin, 98
Empire, 9
Gourmet Dumpling
  House, 97
Hojoko, 151
Mei Mei, 147
O Ya, 86
Pabu, 82
Pagu, 171
Peach Farm, 104
Pho Pasteur, 105
The Q, 103
Ruka, 81
Shojo, 101
Thelonius Monkfish, 173
Uni, 43

Australian
KO Catering and
  Pies, 160

Bar
Carrie Nation, 28
Coppersmith, 76
Deep Ellum, 148
Drink, 6
Harpoon, 14
The Lawn on D, 11
Liberty Hotel, 22
Stanza dei Sigari
  Tunnel, 135
The W, 127

Brazilian
Oliveira's, 162

Brunch
Aquitaine, 57
Beacon Hill Bistro, 26
Lincoln Tavern, 71

Met Back Bay, 47
Metropolis, 52
Oak Long Bar +
  Kitchen, 49
South End Buttery, 58
Trade, 92
Worden Hall, 74

Café
Bao Bao Bakery, 197
Jaho Coffee Roaster
  and Wine Bar, 195
Ogawa Coffee, 196
Panificio, 20
Tatte, 31

Chowder
The No Name, 183
Parker's Restaurant, 185
Union Oyster
  House, 184

Deli
Sam La Grassa, 87

French
Bar Boulud, 42
Deuxave, 46
Frenchie Wine Bistro,
  53
L'espalier, 35
Les Sablons, 180
Ma Maison, 25

Italian
Area Four, 176
Bin 26 Enoteca, 30
Caffe Vittoria, 116
Capo, 72
Cinquecento Roman
  Trattoria, 59
Galleria Umberto, 117
Mamma Maria, 113
Mike's Pastry Shop, 112
Regina Pizzeria, 115
Santarpio's Pizza, 158

Mexican
Angela's Café, 163
Loco, 69
Lone Star, 152
Taquería Jalisco, 159

Middle Eastern
Falafel King, 88

Persian
Lala Rokh, 27

Peruvian
Rincon Limeño, 161

Raw Bar
Island Creek Oyster
  Bar, 143
Row 34, 12
Select Oyster Bar, 39

Rooftop
Colonnade Hotel, 191
Equinox Sports Club
  Boston, 192
Lookout Rooftop Bar,
  187
Rooftop@Revere, 190
Yotel, 188

Seafood
Legal Crossing, 133
Legal Harborside, 16
Il Molo, 121
No Name Restaurant, 3
Reelhouse, 156

Spanish
Toro, 55

Steakhouse
Grill 23, 37
Oliviera's, 162

Wine
Fromage, 77
Haley.Henry, 85

Index

About the Author

JACQUELINE NEVES, known as J. Q. Louise, is a born-and-bred Bostonian. Having grown up dining at the landmark restaurants in town, she appreciates the new flavors that have come to the city. As a social media food and travel influencer, Jacqueline has built relationships with some of Boston's most prominent chefs and restauranteurs and loves to share her culinary adventures with her audience. Her blog, JQLouise.com, offers personal travel stories, curated itineraries, and tips for the globetrotting foodie. In addition to her blog and social channels, Jacqueline has contributed to outlets such as The Food Network, NESN, and AOL Lifestyle, among others.